Live Your Dreams

Let Reality Catch Up

NLP & common sense for
COACHES, MANAGERS
and YOU

ROGER ELLERTON, PHD, CMC

The information in this book is not intended as a substitute for business, medical or psychological counseling. The author and publisher disclaim any responsibility or liability resulting from actions advocated or discussed in this book.

Note for Librarians: A cataloguing record for this book is available from Library and Archives Canada at www.collectionscanada.ca/amicus/index-e.html
ISBN 1-4120-4709-9

PUBLISHING™

Offices in Canada, USA, Ireland and UK

This book was published *on-demand* in cooperation with Trafford Publishing. On-demand publishing is a unique process and service of making a book available for retail sale to the public taking advantage of on-demand manufacturing and Internet marketing. On-demand publishing includes promotions, retail sales, manufacturing, order fulfilment, accounting and collecting royalties on behalf of the author.

Book sales for North America and international:
Trafford Publishing, 6E–2333 Government St.,
Victoria, BC v8t 4p4 CANADA
phone 250 383 6864 (toll-free 1 888 232 4444)
fax 250 383 6804; email to orders@trafford.com
Book sales in Europe:
Trafford Publishing (uk) Limited, 9 Park End Street, 2nd Floor
Oxford, UK ox1 1hh UNITED KINGDOM
phone 44 (0)1865 722 113 (local rate 0845 230 9601)
facsimile 44 (0)1865 722 868; info.uk@trafford.com
Order online at:
trafford.com/04-2517

10 9 8 7 6 5 4 3 2

Acknowledgments

During my life's journey, I have met many wonderful people. I would like to thank all of you who have been part of my life, both in my formative years and now. Each of you in your own way has contributed to my learning about life and about who I can be, and I am ultimately responsible for who I am today. My thanks to those who befriended me and special thanks to those whom I bumped up against or had a disagreement with – you provided me with my greatest opportunities for growth.

I wish to express gratitude to Arlene Prunkl for her excellent editing and proof-reading of this manuscript, and to Fiona Raven, who designed the book cover and interior pages. Their contribution to this book is significant.

As well, I would like to thank John Grinder and Richard Bandler, who first discovered and brought together the information that formed the original basis of NLP, as well as those who followed in their footsteps.

Thank you to all of you who have attended my seminars and to my NLP co-trainers, coaches and friends John Sweetnam, Graham Wright, Denise Wright, Su Thomas and Daniel Beausejour. I have learned much from you and I am sure you will recognize many of your thoughts in this book.

A special thank you to my children, Kim, Deanna, Nick and Matt, who love me as a father and friend even if I do not always satisfy their definition of "dad."

To Donna, my soulmate, who supported me while I took the time to write this book, I extend my deepest appreciation.

And finally, I'm grateful for the support of my parents, William and Irene Ellerton, who unflaggingly stood by me in the best way they knew, and to the maximum of their resources, even though I did not always realize it at the time.

Contents

Preface

For over fifteen years, I have been studying, talking about, using and providing coaching and training services in neuro-linguistic programming (NLP). NLP principles and techniques have had a great impact on my personal communication and the way I perceive and live life. As a Certified Management Consultant and former university professor and executive, I find NLP techniques invaluable in first, assisting me in feeling good about myself and what I choose to do and second, in my conversations and interactions with others as we express our differing points of view and work toward a win-win result. To enhance my knowledge and use of NLP, I have used a number of books as references, yet have not found a single book or small subset of books that fully meets my needs or the needs of those around me. As a result, I have chosen to write my own book with a focus on the following audiences:

- Those who have heard about NLP and wish to learn more.
- Those who are looking for more in life.
- Coaches, members of the helping professions or managers who are looking for new ways and techniques to work with and assist their clients or staff.
- Those who are about to take an NLP seminar and would like to have a solid grounding before beginning.
- Those who have studied NLP and are looking for a basic NLP reference book.

To address these different audiences, in this book, I will speak to you from different perspectives as the situation warrants:

- As a guide to assist you in getting a sense of what NLP is and isn't.
- As a coach to assist you to open up your thinking about yourself and the world around you.
- As a trainer to assist you in understanding and using NLP techniques.
- As a source of knowledge so that you have access to a broad range of NLP tips and techniques.
- As a friend who has and continues to benefit from using NLP.

Throughout the book, I will share my life experiences with you and ask questions of you so that you too can explore new possibilities in your life or in assisting others.

For the most part, the material is presented as if you were in a training session with me. That is, I address the four major learning styles: Why? (discussion), What? (teaching), How? (coaching) and What if? (self-discovery). For those of you who learn best by discussing the reasons why you would use NLP, I often present the material in a discussion format and ask questions of you to stimulate your thinking. Each aspect of NLP and the tips and techniques are presented in enough detail to satisfy those of you who prefer to explore the question "What is NLP?" The basic concepts and techniques of NLP are described in sufficient detail for you know how to apply them in your own life or with others. (I draw your attention to the final paragraphs of section 2.10, A word of caution.) As well, you are provided with sufficient information and questions for you to explore the question "What if I used this in my life or in interactions with others?"

NLP is not a linear subject. It does not lend itself to fit easily into specific chapters. Some of the material might certainly be presented in an earlier chapter and vice-versa. As a result, you will occasionally see references to other chapters. You may find that once you have read the entire book, the material at the beginning of the book becomes richer and more accessible. For those of you using the book as a reference, an index has been provided to meet your needs.

I trust this book will be a valuable resource and I look forward to receiving any observations you may wish to share with me.

Roger Ellerton
Ottawa, Canada

1.

Introduction

> If you can imagine it, you can achieve it. If
> you can dream it, you can become it.
>
> — *William Arthur Ward*

How many of us live our lives according to others' expectations? How many of us have put our lives on hold to accommodate a spouse (current or past), our parents, our children, someone who is needier than us or for our job? How many of us wander through life aimlessly, with one day the same as the next, and with little passion for living or purpose? How many of us know we could do better, if only we knew how to communicate – with ourselves and with others? *Live Your Dreams – Let Reality Catch Up* helps you discover who you are and what really motivates you, and provides you with the knowledge and tools for you to choose what you want in life.

It all begins with communication – the conversation you have with yourself and, of course, the conversations you have with others. Do you tell yourself how wonderful you are, or do you focus on how things can go wrong? Do you tell yourself you deserve success, or do you punish yourself by thinking you do not deserve to succeed? After you have had this conversation with yourself, how does this affect the conversation you have with other people? Do you find that you often prove yourself right, and in doing so, settle for less than you deserve?

NLP (neuro-linguistic programming), the subject of this book, has helped thousands of people to discover the heights of their own potential. Is it your turn? Are you ready?

This book does not pretend to know what is best for you, nor will it tell you how you should live your life. It provides a toolkit for transformation and it is the life manual you didn't get when you were born. It's all about recognizing you have choices – you are constantly choosing. You have the choice of continuing to do what you have always done and getting the same results, or you can choose to do something different.

1.1 WHO WOULD USE THIS BOOK?

Anyone who:

- Is searching for ways and means to personal growth.
- Desires to improve their ability to connect with others.
- Wants to improve communication at home or at work.
- Knows there has to be more to life.
- Interacts with people in any way.

For example, NLP can help:

- **Educators and trainers** to become more resourceful and acquire skills to be more effective with their students.
- **Students** to learn how to cope with the pressures of school.
- **Parents** to interact with their children in a way that leaves everyone feeling seen, heard, respected and loved as individuals.
- **Managers and business people** to improve communication, build stronger and more resourceful teams, be more effective leaders and achieve win-win results.
- **Coaches and helping professions** to become more resourceful and to help their clients discover their own magnificence through new insights, personal resources and skills.

1.2 GETTING THE MOST OUT OF THIS BOOK

This book can be used in a variety of ways: as a reference book; before or after training in NLP; for personal growth; to provide you with additional resources for coping with life; or for you to support your clients, staff or family members. The material has been grouped into eight chapters, each with a particular focus. Due to the non-linear nature of NLP, this is not the only way to group the material. To satisfy a particular need, you may want to make notes and, upon completion of the book, review material from some of the earlier chapters. I strongly recommend marking up the book with your notes in the margins as inspiration strikes you. When you've finished, it will be that much easier to return to passages you found of particular significance.

I have included the words "common sense" in the subtitle, because often after I have explained an NLP concept or technique, people remark, "But isn't that just common sense?" Yes, it is, and until these ideas are brought to your attention, they are outside of your conscious awareness and not always accessible to you.

The concepts in this book are applicable in all areas of your life – work, home, career and recreation. You are limited only by your imagination and your desire to choose the life you want to live.

To get the most out of this book, I encourage you to:

- Have an outcome in mind for reading this book, other than to simply read it. Your outcome may be to improve your communication with others, to discover something significant about yourself or how to develop your skills in assisting others. Take a few moments to write down at least one outcome that you can focus on as you read this book.

- Imagine placing any mental baggage that you have been dragging around, perhaps for years, outside with the trash. You know, the stuff that gets in the way of being who you really want to be and living up to your maximum potential. As you read further into this book, you may find additional mental baggage that you can throw out. Concurrently, you may also wish to clean up and remove unnecessary clutter and baggage in your home or at work.

- Be curious as you read this book. When you come across a new idea, ask yourself: How can I use this? What will happen if I do this? What will happen if I don't do this? Can this be modified to make it more useful in my situation?

- Accept that NLP is a very successful model for understanding human dynamics and change. And that a model is a generalization about some aspect of the world. As you read this book, many generalizations will be proposed. You can focus – negatively – on finding the exception to the rule, or you can accept the general principle and move forward in creating your life.

1.3 SOME IDEAS AS YOU PREPARE TO READ
LIVE YOUR DREAMS – LET REALITY CATCH UP

- Your thoughts and actions in the present create your future.

Just by reading this introduction your thought processes will have been shifted, even if only slightly, which may result in a different conversation and subsequent actions in the coming days.

And what if you were to access additional resources that allow you to change your thoughts about someone significant in your life? Thoughts that allow you to see that person differently and as a result interact with them differently. Would this not create a new and different future for you?

- If you live your life searching for excellence, you will find excellence. If you live your life searching for problems, you will find problems.

- There is a story of the traveler who observed two men working in a stone quarry. One man seemed to be grimly laboring at his work, while the other seemed to have a spring in his step and appeared to be truly enjoying his tasks. The traveler was curious, and asked the first man about the nature of his work. The response that he received was: "I am cutting stone from this quarry to load on that wagon." The traveler then asked the same question of the second man, who replied: "I am building a cathedral!"

  There is a lesson here. Do you view your work as inconsequential or do you see the larger result of your actions? Are you building a cathedral or simply loading stones on a wagon? The choice is yours!

- To paraphrase Captain Kirk of the Starship Enterprise, I invite you to "go where you have not gone before, to explore brave new worlds." The journey is yours and you decide which worlds you wish to visit and those at which you wish to extend your stay. Realize that even for the world or world view that you have today, it is only a visit and it is your choice when to explore other brave new worlds.

As you discover new things about yourself, you will find that there is always more to discover. Personal growth and evolution is a lifelong journey. You can choose whether or not to engage in it and realize that you are always choosing and thus creating the quality of your life.

We are all on a journey. If you are open to it, this book will assist you with your journey, and you will make exciting discoveries along the way – discoveries that will only serve to enhance the remainder of the journey.

2.

Establishing the Foundation

2.1. WHAT IS NLP?

As a certified NLP trainer, I am often asked, "What is NLP?"

The term *NLP* stands for *neuro-linguistic programming* and was coined in the early seventies by John Grinder, an assistant professor of linguistics at the University of California, Santa Cruz, and Richard Bandler, a student of psychology at the university. They began their work by studying Fritz Perls, a psychotherapist and originator of the Gestalt school of therapy, Virginia Satir, a well-known family therapist and Milton Erickson, a world-famous hypnotherapist. Their intention was to model outstanding therapists and identify patterns in order that other practitioners could use these patterns to generate similar results. It may be said that NLP is about identifying excellence through an exploration of patterns, and then devising means for others to use those patterns to achieve similar results, with their clients.

NLP also draws on earlier work, such as Ivan Pavlov's conditioned reflexes (1904). In NLP this is called *anchoring*. NLP takes theoretical results developed by others and makes them available in practical ways to you and me so we can improve our lives and well-being.

NLP is more than just techniques. It is a curiosity about how people who are high achievers accomplish what they actually set out to do. It is also a methodology that assists you in discovering those thinking and communication patterns that prevent you from being successful and shows you how to achieve the results of successful people. That is, NLP is a process of discovering the patterns of excellence of experts, and it makes these effective ways of thinking and communicating available for others to use for their own benefit or to assist others.

NLP had its origins in therapy and is now applied in all areas of human endeavor – education, health, sports, business and, perhaps most importantly, interpersonal relations.

Let us break down and analyze the terms *neuro-linguistic programming*.

Neuro refers to your neurology – sense organs. It is about how you absorb information. For example, you use your eyes to see things in your world. You also experience or perceive events through your other senses: aural (hearing), kinesthetic (tactile touch or emotional feeling), gustatory (taste) and olfactory (smell).

Linguistic refers to the language – pictures, sounds, feelings (kinesthetic), tastes, smells and words – that you use to remember and make sense of a particular experience (or to forecast a future experience). For example, can you recall your breakfast this morning? When you remember having breakfast, can you see a picture in your mind, or can you hear sounds (perhaps a radio was on or you were engaged in a discussion with your family)? What about tastes and smells? And how were you feeling – happy, tired, excited?

Think about a significant event in your near future. Do you envision yourself being successful? Or failing? The pictures, sounds, feelings, tastes, smells and words that you use to describe future experiences have a bearing on what actually happens. You do create your own reality!

Programming refers to your habits, patterns, programs and strategies. If it is a workday, do you follow a particular routine as you get ready for work? Perhaps you like to lie in bed an extra five minutes after the alarm goes off. Do you shower or bathe right away or have breakfast first? If you take time to look at what you do, I am certain you will see a pattern that you follow in getting ready for work. If for some reason you do not follow that pattern, do you find yourself feeling that something is missing?

You have patterns, habits, strategies and programs for everything you do. Some of these patterns serve you, but others do not – resulting in unwanted outcomes. You may be fully aware of some of your patterns. You may become aware of others only when someone else brings them to your attention. And you may choose to quickly forget about these patterns because you want to avoid addressing that part of your life. And there are still other patterns that you are not aware of at all, yet they continue to influence how you look after yourself, communicate with others and perform your daily tasks. If the patterns serve you – that is, generate positive results in your life – great! However, if you find that some patterns do not serve you, would it not be useful to identify those patterns and to change them so they work to your advantage?

Question: Who put your patterns, habits, strategies and programs in place? Of course, you did. So who can change them? Only you. First, you must become aware that you run these patterns. This is one of the biggest benefits of NLP – becoming aware of the patterns, habits, strategies and programs that you have been running unconsciously and then using NLP techniques to change them in order to achieve the outcomes you desire.

2.2. NLP COMMUNICATION MODEL

In simple terms, the NLP communication model is about how you make sense of the world around you and the behaviors that you manifest as a result of your interpretations.

Conscious awareness

It is estimated that your brain receives about four billion nerve impulses every second. Are you consciously aware of all of this information? Of course not. For example, are you aware of how your shirt feels on your back? Unless your shirt is particularly tight or uncomfortable or you have a sunburn, I suspect that you were not aware of how your shirt felt until I mentioned it. Why? Because it was not important at the time and it was filtered out. Of the four billion bits of information, most of it is filtered out. In fact, you are only consciously aware of about 2,000 bits, or about 0.00005 percent of all the potential information. To take in and process more of this information would either drive you crazy or be such a distraction that you could not function.

Filters – deletions, distortions and generalizations

What happens to all of this other information? Your brain filters it from your conscious awareness by:

- Deleting information you consider unimportant (i.e., how your shirt feels on your back). By eliminating extraneous information, you can attend to what is important. Your first impression of someone often sets up deletions, which can get you into trouble or result in missed opportunities.

- Distorting or changing the relationships between experiences. Distorting can provide you with a different view of reality, which can lead you to seeing and experiencing the world differently from others. This may open up new possibilities for you and it may lead to disagreements when your interpretation of reality conflicts with that of others. Simplifying and day-dreaming are examples of distorting.

- Generalizing the information and extending one experience into other situations.

What you actually delete, distort and generalize depends on your beliefs, values, language (the meaning you assign to words), decisions, memories and meta programs. Let us look at a few examples to gain an appreciation of how they work.

Beliefs

Suppose you have a belief that you "can't do anything right." How do you react when someone approaches you and compliments you on your preparation of that report? Depending on the circumstances, you may dismiss, discount or deflect their positive feedback. Internally you may think they have not looked at it in detail and when they do they will find something wrong and change their opinion. Suppose, throughout the day, people tell you that you have done a great job – do you really hear them? If you have negative tapes already playing in your head, it's not likely. And then one person points out that you made a couple of spelling mistakes on page 21. Does this single negative remark resonate with you and verify your belief about yourself? If it does, then from a "filter" perspective, you have deleted and distorted the positive feedback and focused on the negative. What beliefs do you have about yourself, about others, about the world, that limit who you can be or what you can accomplish? What beliefs do you have that open up opportunities for you where others see no possibility?

An example that occurs with great frequency may be found in how you view other people. Let's suggest you believe your boss is incompetent. What, then, do you observe, remember and share with your co-workers? Those times your boss made a mistake or when she did something really well? If you have a pre-conceived negative view, chances are you'll recall only the mistakes.

Language (words)

You may choose to oversimplify or distort how you and your spouse interact by referring to "our relationship." Words are fascinating. They are a form of code to represent your interpretation of something. If you want to have some fun, get a group of people together and have each independently write down five words that for them mean "relationship." I will bet that nobody comes up with the same five words as you do; as a group you may not have any words in common. The word "relationship" is code for what relationship means for you, and you alone, and your spouse quite likely has a completely different meaning for this word. Yet we enter into long and sometimes heated discussions with our loved ones about "our relationship," without ever really discussing what "relationship" means to each other. If this is a topic of concern for you and your spouse, next time you discuss it, you may wish to ask, "How are we relating that is not working for you or supporting you?" You could also ask, "What is working for you?" This will bring to the surface some issues of substance that both of you can work on.

Decisions

You make decisions (i.e., generalize) so you do not have to relearn things every day. If you want to open a door, you do it without thinking. You learned a long time ago – made the generalization – that you grasp the doorknob, twist and pull or push and it opens. You needn't go through the entire process of relearning how to open a door each time. Generalizations are obviously very useful, and they can also get us into trouble. In an experiment, researchers put the doorknob on the same side of the door as the hinge, then filled the room with adults. What do you imagine happened when the adults attempted to leave the room? They would approach the door, grasp the doorknob, twist and then push or pull the door open. Of course, it would not open. As a result, the adults concluded that the door was locked and, therefore, they were locked in the room. Young children, on the other hand, who had not yet made the generalization about the doorknob, simply walked up to the door, pushed on it and exited the room. The adults, because of their generalizations, created a reality of being locked in the room when in fact they were not. How many of your decisions or generalizations about your spouse, your boss, your circumstances at work or about the world in general leave you "locked in," when others are open to new ideas?

Internal representations

Do you remember having breakfast this morning? How do you remember it? Do you see a picture in your mind, or are there smells or tastes? Were there sounds – perhaps in your mind you can hear a radio? To remember an event, your mind uses pictures, sounds, feelings, tastes, smells and words. These perceptions of your "outside world" are called *internal representations* and are a function of your filters. Your perceptions are what you consider to be "real" or, in other words, your reality.

If you and I have breakfast together, our internal representations or perception of the occasion will most likely be similar in some ways and different in others, depending on what is important or unimportant to each of us (our filters). Breakfast is not very controversial. But what about our views on the war in Iraq? Given our different backgrounds, we may perceive this controversial war very differently with significantly different reactions or behaviors.

Filters

Have you ever gone with a friend to see a movie, sat next to each other, watched exactly the same movie, yet one of you thought it was the best movie you'd ever seen and the other thought it a waste of time? How could that happen? It is quite simple. You and your friend filtered the information differently, employing different beliefs, values and decisions. Based on these beliefs and your previous experiences, you each perceived the movie differently; hence you behaved differently in your reaction to it.

Filters serve to protect you in some ways. Based on your perception of the world, there is a positive intent, although this positive intent may not be obvious or even logical according to another person's view of the world. And you may not be consciously aware of the perceived positive benefit. An understanding of filters helps to explain why not everyone experiences the world the same way, nor wants the same rewards from life, nor reacts in the same manner to a specific event. This does not make one of us right or the other wrong; it is simply that we see things differently.

You may find it interesting to examine the origin of your filters. Who put those filters in place? Recall the same person who put your habits, strategies and generalizations in place. Of course, it is you. You chose these filters, based on what happened in your family as you grew up, the teachings of your church (or the absence of church), the beliefs and values in the part of the country in which you lived, and the decisions you made about the world (i.e., a safe place or a dangerous place). If your filters are not creating the results that you desire, you are the only person who can change them. The first step is to become consciously aware of the filters you have created and what kind of reality and results they are returning for you.

Internal representations and behaviors

Would you like to see the effect internal representations have on your behaviors? Think of a magical event in your life – perhaps a time when you were truly happy and laughing. Close your eyes and get a picture of this event in your mind, bring in any sounds, feelings, tastes and smells. Fully experience the event in your mind. Notice the effect it has on your state. By recalling these internal representations, are you beginning to feel the magic of that event? Once you have fully experienced this event in your mind, notice whether there were any changes in your physiology. Perhaps as a result of these memories or internal representations and the resulting change in your psychological state, you now have a smile on the face, are starting to chuckle, are sitting up straighter or perhaps breathing deeper. This is a sure sign that your physiology changed in some way, yet I did not ask you to change your physiology, did I? It changed of its own accord. What this demonstrates is that the pictures, sounds and linguistic associations that you create in your mind influence your state. These, in turn, influence your physiology and as a result, your choice of words, the tone of voice you use and the behaviors you manifest.

Now, sit up straight, put a big smile on your face, tilt your head up slightly and breathe deeply. While you do that, attempt to feel sad. I am almost certain that you cannot feel sad without changing your physiology (i.e. with shallow breathing and rounded shoulders). This illustrates that your physiology influences your state – whether you feel sad or happy – which in turn influences your internal representations. Next time you are feeling sad or down, the best antidote is to participate in some physical activity such as a brisk walk or other form of mild exercise.

Another example: Suppose you believe that your boss is the part of the horse that is over the fence last. You are on your way to see your boss, and in your mind you think, "What an ass!" Not only do you think it, but you have internal representations in the form of pictures, sounds and feelings of previous events that prove it – these are your reality. With these internal representations at the forefront of your mind, what do you think your physiology will be like when you walk into his office? What about your tone of voice or the words you use? Given those behaviors, do you think he will support your idea or do what you suggest? Most likely not! And what has he done? Proved once more that he is indeed a horse's ass.

Suppose one of your co-workers thinks this same boss is a perfect example of leadership and mentorship. What kind of internal representations do you think your colleague is making in her mind about the boss? What will her physiology, her tone of voice, or the words she uses demonstrate? And what about the results that she gets with the boss? Because of your different perceptions – your internal representations – you each created different results and hence different realities.

Based on your previous experiences and decisions, you filter information from the world around you. The resulting internal representations are how you perceive the world – your reality – and this drives your state and your behaviors, which serve to reinforce that your perception of the world is "correct."

I have found that one of the benefits of NLP is discovering the filters I have in place and how they affect what I see, hear and feel, how I react to others and what I create in my life. Once I become aware of those filters that do not serve me, I can choose consciously or with the help of NLP techniques to modify or remove them.

> Some studies suggest that less than 50 percent of what we "see" is actually based on information entering our eyes. The remaining 50 percent plus is pieced together out of our expectations of what the world should look like (and perhaps out of other sources such as reality fields).
>
> – Michael Talbot, The Holographic Universe, HarperPerennial, 1992, p. 163

2.3. THE STRUCTURE OF REALITY

What is reality? Why is it that some people see a task or a goal as possible (within their reality) and others completely discount it?

Your perception of the world is your reality

For the NLP communication model, we discussed how you filter information based on your beliefs, values, memories and meta programs. As a result of this filtering, you have a perception of the world that you call reality. There is a saying: "If you wish to change your life, first you must change the way you perceive your life." Your perception of the world is your own reality.

To get a better understanding of reality and how it affects your life, consider the following: Suppose the circle in Figure 1 represents all possible knowledge – all that has been discovered and all that will be discovered. One piece of this circle represents "what you know you know" – you know your name, where you live and so forth. Another piece of the circle represents "what you know you don't know" – you know there is something called scuba diving, but you do not know any of the details or how to do it. These two pieces represent what you call reality (or your perception of reality). The rest of the circle is "what you don't know you don't know" and is, at this time, outside of your perception (reality). Simply because it is not part of your awareness or reality doesn't mean that it does not have an effect on your life. For example, until I tell you, are you aware that you have a new stomach lining every five days? (Deepak Chopra, *Perfect Health: The Complete Mind/Body Guide*, Revised and Updated Edition, 2000.)

The larger your reality, the more choices you have in life

If you were to step out of your reality to, say, the green dot (i.e., do something you have never done before with no idea of how it will turn out), how might you feel? For example, if you had never been to Japan, were not a world traveler, could not speak Japanese and found yourself instantaneously transported to a street corner in downtown Tokyo, how might you feel? Fearful, confused, apprehensive or anxious? Or it might happen that your mind goes blank. (On the other hand, if your reality is to travel to different places and experience the culture with the local inhabitants, you may experience this quite differently). What is your typical reaction when you have these feelings of fear, confusion, apprehension or anxiety? Many people rush back to something they know and perceive to be safe – their familiar reality – and shut down any process of exploring new ideas about the world or about themselves. If you are to expand your reality and your potential in life, it is necessary to explore "what you don't know you don't know."

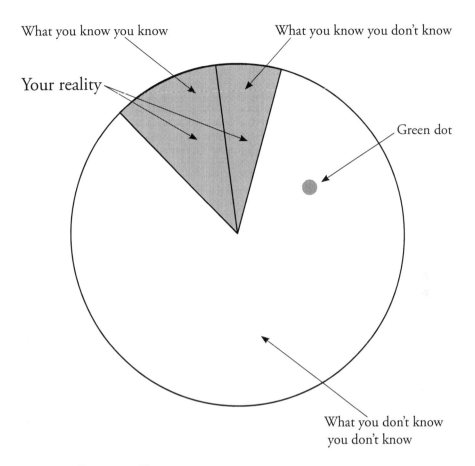

FIGURE 1: YOUR REALITY AND STEPPING OUTSIDE OF IT

A "green dot" moment

When students in our NLP training sessions discover new things about themselves or explore their beliefs and values, sometimes they find themselves fearful, confused, apprehensive or anxious. I point out to them that this is a good thing, as it means they are exploring new aspects of themselves. How can they be manifesting these emotions about something they already know? As they become more comfortable exploring who they are and trusting in themselves, it is common to hear them say, "I am having a green dot moment," or "Wow! I just had a green dot moment and learned something very valuable about myself or how I perceive the world."

A *green dot* moment can be a fragment of inspiration, a flash of brilliance or insight, or simply a feeling of peace and contentment that all is well and right with your world.

The next time you have any of these feelings of self-doubt, first make sure you are safe, then relax. Breathing deep (often we tend to hold our breath at times like this, which only makes the situation worse), let your mind explore the nature of these feelings. You may discover new insights about who you are, your beliefs and values, your strategies for achieving what you want in life or how you can better manage that everyday situation that causes you problems and achieve different, more desirable results.

Appreciating another person's reality

Let's assume that you and I grew up in different cultures with different religions, different beliefs and values, and for argument's sake, that we have completely different perceptions of the world. This is illustrated in the extreme in Figure 2. What is the potential for us to agree and work together? If we both hold fast to our beliefs and values, and are not willing to explore new ideas (have you ever meet anyone like that?), then we would undoubtedly be continually disagreeing. On the other hand, what would happen if you decided to explore my reality? You needn't agree with me, only appreciate and respect that I can have different beliefs and values from yours, and avoid judging which of our belief/value systems is right or wrong. At first you may find my reality confusing; however, if you continued to explore it with me, you have the potential to expand your own awareness (bring more choices into your life), assist me in being more tolerant of your reality and open up the possibility for us to improve our communication with each other. In being flexible in your approach and able to explore ideas outside of your reality, you have the potential to create a life of much more depth for yourself, and to assist others in their self-development at the same time. This is part of what is meant by organizational experts who say we should encourage diversity in the workplace.

How would your life and the results you are currently achieving in your life be different if you were to accept that members of your family, colleagues or neighbors see the world differently than you do; that is, they have a different reality? All that's required of you is to choose to be inquisitive and appreciate their different perspectives.

What you don't know you know

Looking at Figure 1, you'll see there is another part to the circle that we haven't yet discussed: "what you don't know you know." This can have many interpretations. For example, many adults have painful memories from childhood that they have chosen to suppress. Or children may be culturally conditioned to take on certain roles and not others (boys are to follow in the footsteps of their fathers or young girls are told they can not do mathematics or be engineers or

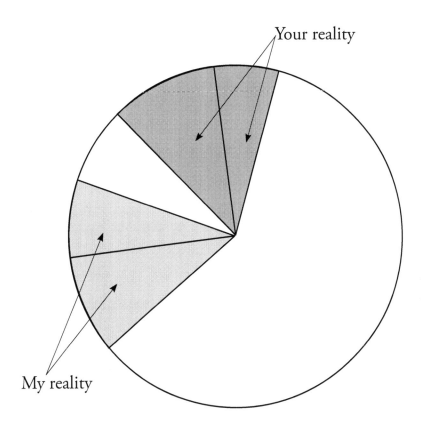

Figure 2: Appreciating different realities

airline pilots). What impact does this have on your reality and your perceived choices in your life?

Innovation is exploring "what you don't know you don't know"

Finally, let's talk briefly about innovation. This can be your own personal innovation, innovation in the workplace or within society. Referring to Figure 1, think about where the innovative new ideas will come from. Will they be found in things "we already know we know?" Most decidedly not. From "what we know we don't know?" In this case, there is some potential for small advances. Or will the innovative ideas come from stepping into "what we don't know we don't know" or "what we don't know we know?" Yes – here, ultimately, is where the opportunity lies for big breakthroughs.

NLP tools and techniques can assist you in expanding your reality in a safe, resourceful and respectful way. Once you are able to do this for yourself or with the aid of a coach, you will have the knowledge and experience, in turn, to assist others.

> Reality leaves a lot to the imagination.
>
> *– John Lennon*

2.4. THE FIVE STEPS FOR SUCCESS

Most successful people follow (either consciously or unconsciously) five simple steps:

1. Have an outcome
2. Take action
3. Use sensory acuity
4. Be flexible
5. Have a physiology and psychology of excellence

Taking one, two, three or four of these steps is just not good enough. What use is it to have an outcome if you do not take action? Nor is it useful to take action if you are not paying attention to the results you are creating. And how often have you missed achieving something important by not being flexible? And then you wonder why your life is the same today as it was yesterday, last month or last year.

1. **Have an outcome**

   In NLP, we prefer to refer to a goal as an *outcome*. This removes some of the pressure and finality conventionally attached to the word *goal*.

   You need to have an outcome in mind for everything you do. Choosing to do nothing or to wander through life is an outcome itself. Realize you chose this path and ask yourself, "How well is this outcome serving me?" If you have not set an outcome for today and you meet a friend who has, most likely your friend will enlist you to help her get what she wants. And you may (silently or otherwise) become angry at her for taking advantage of you, when in reality you set the stage for what happened. Be conscious of the choices you are making in your life and the consequences or rewards that follow.

   What is your outcome for reading this book? If it is simply to read this book, you may congratulate yourself – you are on your way to achieving it! Or you may wish to consider the following outcome: As you read each section, find at least one idea that, were you to adopt it, would change your life for the better.

When you are ready, why not set other outcomes that you would like to achieve, in the areas of health, relationships, career, family and spirituality?

2. Take action

Many people with a clear outcome do not take action to achieve it. How many times have you heard a friend (or even yourself) talk passionately about building or achieving something, and yet they never fully commit to it and it remains but a dream, year after year.

To illustrate, suppose my outcome is to take a vacation to part of the country that I have not seen before. Unless I take action, such as getting in my car – or taking the bus, train or airplane – this will simply remain an outcome that I would like to achieve, perhaps next week, next month or next year. I will never achieve it if I don't take action.

> Thinking will not overcome fear but action will.
> – *W. Clement Stone*

3. Use your sensory acuity

You need to be continually aware of your outcome; as well, you need some form of measure to know whether you are making progress toward it. If you don't, how will you know if or when you have actually achieved it? Perhaps you are going in the wrong direction!

Turning to the example of taking a vacation, assume I am driving along the highway, when a signpost appears which clearly indicates I am off course. I can take note of this piece of information or, as some of us do, I can choose to ignore it and continue on my journey. Have you ever done that? I know I have, particularly when I have not been paying attention to what is important to me and what is happening in my life, or when I am not prepared to admit I made a mistake.

4. Be flexible

Some of us see the signposts of life clearly, yet we choose not to admit we need to change course or alter our behaviors. Other times, we may stop and berate these signposts of life for telling us something we don't want to hear, before continuing in the same misguided direction and blindly hoping things will all work out.

In my example, I can choose to notice that I have driven in the wrong direction, and hope that if I persist long enough in this one direction, everything will eventually work out. Alternatively, I can become aware of the signpost and decide to explore what other options are available to me.

5. **Have a physiology and psychology of excellence**
   Recall from the NLP communication model that your thoughts (internal representations) affect your physiology and your physiology affects your thoughts. In your mind, have thoughts (pictures, sounds, feelings, tastes and smells) of having achieved your outcome, while adopting a supporting physiology.

   This reminds me of an experience reported to me by a student in one of my classes. He had a friend who, after graduation from college, wanted to be an executive in a financial institution. After graduation, the best job he could find was in the mailroom in a financial institution. This did not deter him at all. Every day he showed up for work in a suit and tie and carried himself as if he were already an executive – for in his mind, he was an executive, one who just happened to be getting a little experience in the mailroom. Do you think he was noticed? Indeed he was. Do you think he advanced in the financial institution? Indeed he did! A couple of years later, management recognized what he had known all along and officially appointed him to an executive position.

2.5. NLP PRESUPPOSITIONS

The foundation for NLP is a set of presuppositions (beliefs) about ourselves and the world we live in. These presuppositions also serve as principles to guide how we live our lives. Depending on the presenter, the number of NLP presuppositions and the wording may vary, but the basic intent is the same.

The following are my favorites. You may find some of them are already part of your life. You may also find one or more of them confusing or unrealistic. In this case, they may be part of "what you don't know you don't know." There may be value for you to step into this belief and see what you can discover about yourself and what else is possible.

1. **You cannot not communicate.**
   Often we think we communicate only when we say or write something. This is not so. Consider the following: You are in a staff meeting sitting off to one side, with your arms folded and an angry look on your face, and you are not participating in the discussion at all. Or you have chosen not to respond to telephone and e-mail messages in a timely fashion, or at all. Even no communication sends a message, and it is often not a positive one. And who are you really hurting?

   Through your tone of voice, actions, facial expressions, gestures and body language, you are always communicating. Take time to step back and see the impact of your actions on the larger system. Is this really the impression you wish to create or the message you wish to convey?

2. The map is not the territory.

I live in Ottawa, Canada. To get an idea of where places are located in Ottawa, I can refer to a street map. The map is not Ottawa, but a visual representation. Someone else, with a different purpose in mind, could draw an entirely different representation (i.e., a topographical map) of Ottawa. Both would represent Ottawa and give a different perspective.

In a similar way, you remember your experiences by creating maps (internal representations) in your mind. These maps are made up of pictures, sounds, feelings, tastes, smells and words. As noted earlier, these internal representations depend on your filters – your beliefs, values and decisions.

Your map of an event is not the event. How you choose to represent the map in your mind is what gives meaning to the event. If you and I had attended the same event, our maps might be quite different, depending on our filters. Later, when we discuss the event, we may disagree on certain points. We are not really disagreeing on the event itself or what happened at the event. Rather we have differing interpretations (maps) of the event. In other words, our differences are based on what we experienced, which depends upon our filters. So the real discussion is about our differences in beliefs, values and decisions. For example, suppose you believe your boss is a horse's ass. What sort of representation or map will you make of your meeting with him? Will you tend to focus on those things that prove your point? If I am in the same meeting, and I think he is wonderful, how will my memory and map of the meeting differ from yours?

Your senses take in raw data from your environment and that raw data has absolutely no meaning whatsoever other than the meaning or "map" you choose to give it. If you were to choose a different meaning, this would change your experience of that event.

People act and react according to their map of reality, not to reality itself. NLP is about changing these maps – not reality – to obtain different results from life.

3. Respect for the other person's model of the world.

We each have our own interpretation of reality – our own view or model of the world. Our interpretations may be quite similar to or differ vastly from another person's.

We each map our experience of the world differently, because we all have different sets of experiences and filters. You may not understand or agree with my behavior. However, if you had a similar upbringing to mine, you may well have adopted similar beliefs, values, decisions and interpretations of reality as mine.

You do not have to agree with your colleague's model of the world, only respect that he may see, hear, feel and interpret the world differently than you do. As a result, he may be motivated by different values, make different choices and hence behave differently. It's not personal. He simply has a different perspective of the world.

The Golden Rule states: "Do unto others as you would have others do unto you." Perhaps the Platinum Rule should state: "Do unto others by respecting their model of the world."

4. The system or person with the most flexibility of behavior will have the most influence on the system.

Have you ever been stuck in life, doing the same things repeatedly and each time expecting to get a different result? This is the widely known definition of insanity. If you want your life to be different, doing the same things more often, harder, louder, is not the way to change it. You must choose to do something different. If you try one key in a lock and it doesn't fit, would you keep trying the same key repeatedly? Or would you be flexible and try other keys until you find the one that works?

It is the same for your life. Be flexible and explore different behaviors and strategies to unlock what you truly want in life or who you are destined to be.

At work, you perhaps have noticed two types of people. One person may be very inflexible, trying to control everything. He lives under the illusion that he is in charge. In reality, his colleagues are simply finding work-arounds in order to avoid dealing with him. Then there is the other kind of person, whom people enjoy talking with and helping. Why? Because by being flexible in her behavior, she is able to communicate with everyone. People see her as a valuable and an asset to their team and their lives.

If you are a parent, consider the following related thought: There are no resistant children, only inflexible adults.

5. The meaning of communication is the response it produces.

Your intended communication is not always what is understood by the other person. It does not matter what your intention is, what matters are the results you generate from your words, tone of voice, facial expressions and body language. By being flexible, you can change how you are communicating until you achieve your desired result.

Consider the following situation. As a man, I notice a female co-worker is wearing a new dress, so I decide to pay her a compliment (my sincere intention). I say to her, "My, you look terrific in that dress." However, her reaction isn't what I expected. She seems annoyed and leaves the room. I do not know what is going on in her mind, but obviously she heard my message very differently from what I had intended. Perhaps in her model of the world and through her filters, she felt I was "hitting on her" or being suggestive. The next time I see her, I can continue with the same behavior, or simply ignore her and harbor all manner of bad thoughts about her. Or I can recognize that my remark did not produce the effect I had intended and find different ways to communicate with her so that we can have a productive working relationship.

6. **There is no failure, only feedback.**
You do something and it doesn't work out the way you had planned. How often do you interpret this as failure? Next time, you might view it simply as information you can use to change what you are doing in order to move closer to the results you desire.

> I have not failed. I've just found
> 10,000 ways that won't work.
>
> *— Thomas Alva Edison, scientist and inventor*

How would your life change if you viewed failure simply as feedback – an opportunity to learn how *not* to do something and become flexible in developing new ways to achieve your intended outcome?

How different would your job be if failure were viewed as feedback? Would you and others be more inclined to explore new ways to get your work done more efficiently and effectively, with more fun?

> It is better to have enough ideas for
> some of them to be wrong, than to be
> always right by having no ideas at all.
>
> *— Edward de Bono*

7. **Every behavior has a positive intention.**
No matter how strange, hurtful or inappropriate a person's behavior may seem to you, for the person engaging in that behavior, it makes sense in their model of the world and is predicated upon satisfying a positive intention for them.

The key is to appreciate that there is a positive intention behind the other person's behavior. This does not mean that you must view the other person's behavior as positive or acceptable. On the contrary, you may find it quite distasteful. You need to look behind the behavior to discover the positive intention or, if it's not apparent, look for an intention that makes sense in their reality. This intention may be for themselves, for you or for someone else. Once you have an understanding of their intention, you can explore alternative ways to help the person achieve it.

As an example, let's say you are having a discussion with someone and he begins to raise his voice, yell, knock things off the table and run from the room. From your perspective, this certainly cannot be viewed as positive behavior. What could possibly be the positive intention behind this kind of behavior? Now look at it from the other person's perspective. Given his background – his model of the world – perhaps he felt unsafe or over-whelmed in the conversation with you. Given the resources he had avail-able at that moment, this may have been the only option he felt he had in order to create some space or to flee to a place of greater safety.

What can you do to avoid a similar result next time? Using the NLP pre-suppositions, you can accept what happened as feedback, respect his model of the world, explore the possible positive intentions behind his behavior and look at other ways to achieve your outcome while satisfying his posi-tive intention. In other words, be flexible.

Now consider other possibilities. Could you use this approach to improve your relationship with you boss? Your colleagues? Your family? Your chil-dren? Your spouse?

It is useful to take stock of your own behaviors on a regular basis. That is, no-tice the results you are achieving, identify the positive intention behind these behaviors and ask, "Is there a better way to achieve my positive intention?"

A similar way to express this presupposition is: People always do what they believe is right and what works best for their own reality.

8. **Everyone does the best they can with the resources available to them.**
    Similar ways to phrase this presupposition are: "there are no unresourceful people, only unresourceful states of mind," or "this is the best choice avail-able to this person given the circumstances as they see them."

    In NLP, we believe people already have the resources they need to suc-ceed. However, their model of the world (with its limiting beliefs and constraints) may limit them from seeing what is really possible or prevent them from accessing their full capabilities and resources. Or they may be in a temporary state of mind (overwhelmed, sad, angry) that prevents them from fully accessing all of their resources. In these situations, a person may make certain decisions or take actions that, from another viewpoint, are much less than they are capable of and that may even be experienced as hurtful.

With hindsight, that person could have done many things differently, but it was deemed the best choice at the time. We do not always make the "right" decision or take the "right" action; simply, decisions and actions are taken based on what resources we have available to us at the time.

If your mother or father did not know how to love themselves or one another, how would it be possible for them to teach you to love yourself? Your parents were doing the best they could with the understanding, awareness and knowledge they had at that time. They could only teach you what they themselves knew. If they had been raised differently, or had access to resources that helped them to love themselves, they would have been equipped with an expanded model of the world and thus more choice in the behaviors they exhibited and taught.

NLP is about expanding your reality and gaining more choices.

9. **You are in charge of your mind and therefore your results.**
   It was you who chose the filters – the beliefs, values and decisions – that determine your maps, your model of the world and how you experience different events. It is also you who can change these filters to gain a different perspective on the world and thus reap the benefits of potentially significantly different results.

You can simply read the above presuppositions or you can begin to put them into action and make them a way of life. In doing so, you have the opportunity to change your reality, your results and your life! Here are two methods you may wish to consider:

1) Begin to incorporate these presuppositions into your life by selecting a different presupposition each day. Read it over carefully and during the day, at work and at home, notice when this presupposition applies. Then consider what other courses of action are available to you in any given situation in order to achieve the most positive results from life.

2) Identify a situation in the past in which you did not perform as well as you could have. Take each presupposition one at a time and review the situation from each of these perspectives. As you do, notice what you can learn about yourself, about others and what other choices are available to you to obtain a different result – should a similar circumstance arise in the future.

2.6. ARE YOU AT CAUSE OR EFFECT?

How do you live your life? At cause or at effect? It is important to be aware of this distinction. It is the rare individual who always lives his or her life *at cause*;

however, far too many of us live a large portion of our lives *at effect* – responding to the whims, desires or emotional states of others.

Being at cause means that you are decisive in creating what you want in life and take responsibility for whatever you achieve. You see the world as a place of opportunity and you move toward achieving what you desire. If things are not unfolding as you would like, you take action and explore other possibilities. Above all, you know you have choice in what you do and how you react to people and events.

If you are at effect, you may blame others or circumstances for your bad moods, for what you have not achieved or for the disarray of your life in general. You may feel powerless or depend on others in order for you to feel good about yourself or about life. You may think, "If only my spouse, my boss, my co-workers, my parents, my children understood me and helped me achieve my dreams or did what I wanted or what is best for me, then life would be great." If you wait and hope for things to be different or for others to provide you with results or happiness, you are at effect, or a victim of circumstances. And really, how satisfying is that? How satisfying do you think it is for others to be around you? Believing that someone else is responsible for your happiness or your different moods is very limiting and gives this person mystical powers over you, which can cause both you and the other person a great deal of anguish.

Being at cause means you have choices in your life – you can choose what is best for you while ensuring the choice is ecological (see chapter 2.8) for those around you, in your community and your society. That is, you consider the consequences of your actions on others, while not taking responsibility for their emotional well-being. Believing you are responsible for the emotional well-being of someone else places a heavy burden upon you and can cause a great deal of stress.

Those who live their lives at effect often see themselves as victims with no choices whatsoever. The truth is that they do have choices but have chosen not to take action. They are simply reactive to whatever is thrust upon them.

Emotions such as guilt, fear, anxiety and resentment are the result of being at effect. People at effect tend to blame others and do not take responsibility for their actions. Emotions such as these can wear heavily on a person's body and life, and can be the root cause of many physical and personal issues.

Do I always live my life at cause? No, not a chance; the great majority of the time I do live at cause. When I don't, I use NLP techniques to help me to get back on track, to explore other ways to achieve my outcomes or to ask others for help – without being a victim to their answers.

Each morning when you get up, you can either ask yourself, "I wonder what my day will bring," or "What do I choose to bring to my day?" The choice is yours.

2.7. POWER OF THOUGHT

Look around you. Perhaps you see a chair. This chair is real and exists in time and space. Yet before it came into being, it first existed as a thought. In fact, everything in the room existed as a thought at some point in someone's mind. Who you are today and the reality you have created are a result of your thoughts – your thoughts about what is possible and what's not. These thoughts are influenced by your spirituality – your purpose – who you see yourself being, and your beliefs and values.

It is said that a person has over 60,000 thoughts every day. That's over forty thoughts a minute! Yet, of the 60,000 thoughts you have today, ninety percent of these are the same as the 60,000 you had yesterday and the day before, leaving little room for new thoughts. No wonder life can seem tedious at times. Unless you start to think differently, you are destined to continue to create and repeat the same old reality every day. Is it not time to change your thoughts, live your dreams and let reality catch up?

Most of our thoughts and actions are habits, and we go through the same motions each day, with little change in our behaviors or outlook. What would happen if you challenged these habits or customs? If you were to step out of your comfort zone and explore new ideas or new ways of doing things? Would your life not change as a result?

Often our thoughts are about not measuring up, being incapable or inadequate, avoiding failure or beating ourselves up because we did not say or do the right thing. Just as thought preceded the creation of the chair, your thoughts precede the reality that you create for yourself.

The future lies ahead of you, determined by your current thoughts. These are the only thoughts over which you have any control. What thoughts will you choose for yourself that will be the cause of a different future for you?

Thought is a form of energy. Does this energy propel you forward or hold you back? You have a choice about the thoughts you think. How many times in the past have you chosen to disregard your positive thoughts and focus on your negative thoughts? At this moment, if you were to be at cause and to focus on your positive thoughts while discounting your negative thoughts, how would your life change?

> You become what you think about.
>
> – *Earl Nightingale*

To realize your dreams, pay attention to what is happening around you. Be curious. Notice how your thoughts about yourself, your thoughts about others and your thoughts about what others may be thinking of you influence what you are able to achieve. Start to think, see and experience things, people, places and events in new ways. Recognize what happens when you begin to think differently about yourself and what you are capable of achieving.

2.8. SYSTEMS

A system is defined as a group of interacting, interrelated or interdependent elements forming a complex whole. Our bodies are systems, composed of subsystems such as the digestive, immune, endocrine, respiratory, circulatory, reproductive and nervous systems. And each of these systems is made up of other subsystems. Similarly, we are a subsystem of many different larger systems – family, work, community and social. Each system is influenced by the larger system and its subsystems. For example, if your work environment is chaotic, this may cause you stress. Stress will affect your endocrine system, which is a collection of glands that secrete hormones that influence almost every organ and function in your body. On the other hand, if you have an illness, this can limit your capabilities and hence your activities within the larger family or work system. The functions of this larger system may break down due to the dysfunction of your smaller subsystems.

If part of a system changes, other related parts of the system will also change to maintain balance in the system. If you have heart problems, for instance, other organs will change to compensate for this diminished functionality. In an alcoholic family, other family members may take on co-dependent behaviors, which in turn influence the creation of yet other systems – a high percentage of children from alcoholic families become addicts themselves or marry alcoholics.

Each of us is a living system. If one part of the system is changed, other parts must adapt. Given this fact, consider the following. What if you misinterpreted a significant past event – an event that led you to make limiting decisions about yourself, about others, about the world in which you live? Given the resources you have as an adult and what you know today, what if you were to reassess that event and were to come to a different understanding or decision? Would this not change how you perceive and respond to life as well as change how you will live your life in the future? This idea of conscious awareness, change and subsequent growth is addressed throughout this book.

Ecology

Ecology is the relationship between subsystems and with the larger system. In NLP, before making a change or committing to an outcome, it's important to check the ecology of the proposed change. That is, you need to be consciously aware of the effects and consequences of your proposed actions on yourself, your health, your family, your colleagues, your employer, your community and society. This does not mean you give in to others' demands or needs. It simply means that before committing to a new course of action, you are aware of the consequences of not proceeding, as well as the consequences of your proposed actions. You may then wish to explore whether there is another way in which you can achieve the same desired result for yourself while minimizing the perceived negative consequences on your health or for other people in your life.

2.9. FRAMES

Successful managers, consultants and contractors set the scope or frame of a project so that all involved know what is included and excluded.

In a similar way, *frames* in NLP provide a context, a focus or guidance for your thoughts and actions.

A "frame of reference" is useful for providing a focus for your activities, for ensuring you are congruent (see page 67 for more about personal congruence), for providing a context in which you can assess your progress, for exploring other possibilities or for ensuring a common understanding.

We can obtain different perspectives of an event or situation by viewing it through different frames. Further along in the book we will discuss *reframing*. Reframing is about changing or expanding our frames of reference. Sometimes we define our frames too narrowly, thus locking ourselves into behaviors that do not support us. This causes us to miss seeing other opportunities and possibilities.

Examples of frames are as follows:

Outcome frame

An *outcome frame* provides a focus for what you want to achieve. It allows you to consider the ensuing effects and the resources required to achieve your outcome. You need to determine an outcome for all your activities.

As a consultant, I work with a number of different organizations. I frequently hear people say, "We need to have a meeting." That decision results in a group of people meeting for one or two hours or perhaps half a day. Yet when they exit the meeting, they are often not clear on what has been accomplished or what is expected of them. Why? Because the outcome was simply to "have a meeting"! If this has happened to you, instead of being frustrated, you might congratulate yourself for achieving your outcome. Next time, you should realize that you need to set a more substantial outcome.

Clearly defined outcomes provide you with a context for making decisions and assessing your behaviors. Without these clear definitions, you may limit your accomplishments, take on too much and become overwhelmed – or simply fail to accomplish your dreams.

Problem frame

A *problem frame* is the opposite of an outcome frame. A problem frame focuses upon what is wrong or needs to be fixed rather than what is sought after. This frame is useful in discovering potential problems that can derail a project or outcome. Some people focus solely on their outcome, not considering or taking stock of potential problems.

Evidence frame

This frame is part of the outcome frame and is useful to consider separately. Simply, how will you know when you have achieved your outcome? What will you see, hear, feel or experience?

The *evidence frame* is used as a gauge to assess how well you are progressing toward your outcome and to know when your outcome has been achieved. As a result of observing the evidence, you will know whether corrective action should be taken or whether a new or modified outcome should be set.

Ecology frame

A person who pursues his outcome without regard for the impact on other systems (i.e., body systems, family, work environment, community) has not taken into account the *ecology frame*. For example, going on a diet may result in an attractive body, but is the diet good for your immune system? At your job, what is the effect of the outcome on your colleagues, and can you mitigate any negative effects? Is the outcome you desire for your home life compatible with the needs and expectations of your neighbors and community? Is this outcome congruent with other outcomes you have planned?

"As if" frame

This frame has many applications and is based upon acting *as if* a desired state or outcome has been realized or *as if* someone else is giving you information:

- The best way to achieve your outcome is to act as if you have already achieved it – live your dreams now and let reality to catch up.

- When negotiating or problem solving, you can explore other possibilities by saying, "Let's proceed as if I have agreed to this demand or take your proposed course of action. What would you do for me, or what would happen as a result?"

- If a key person is missing from a meeting, you may say, "Let's act as if Sue were present. What would she suggest?"

- For project planning, you may wish to act as if the project has been successfully completed and then working backward, ask what steps were necessary to reach this outcome. This approach may highlight some important information that is not obvious when planning forward from the present.

- When modeling an expert – an important part of NLP – you may choose to act as if you are that person by putting yourself in their shoes. This is called the *second position*, and it will help you to gain further insights into their thoughts and behaviors.

Backtrack frame

This frame can be used to check agreement and understanding during and at the conclusion of a meeting, to update a new arrival or to restart a discussion. Backtracking is accomplished by reviewing the available information using the keywords and tonality of those who brought the information forward.

We all filter information differently and may come to significantly different conclusions. Backtracking is a way to ensure everyone has the same understanding of what has been discussed and decided. It helps to maintain a course toward the desired outcome.

Two other frames that you may come across are:

- **Relevancy Frame:** Determining if a behavior, comment or question is pertinent to achieving an agreed outcome.

- **Open Frame:** An opportunity for people to provide any comments or ask any questions relevant to the topic under consideration.

2.10. OTHER FOUNDATION PIECES

This section provides the remaining foundation pieces that will support your understanding and enjoyment of the material in this book.

Be aware of using negatives

Your unconscious mind cannot process a negative. Your unconscious mind first brings up the thought without the negation and then "puts a line through it."

If I ask you to not think of a pink elephant, what do you think of? A pink elephant!

Your children arrive home from school. You say to them, "Don't eat the cookies." Your children had not even thought of cookies until you said this. Now you have a ten-minute discussion with your children about eating cookies. How often do you hear people stating what not to do – radio announcers telling us "Don't change the station," or a well-wisher saying to us, "Don't be nervous." In order to follow these instructions, what do you first think of? Would it not be better to say, "stay tuned" or "be calm"?

By expressing what you don't want, you raise your awareness of exactly this and significantly increase the chances of it happening. Suppose you are a golfer and between you and the green is a body of water. What do you say to yourself? "Don't hit the ball into the water." Where is your focus? And what are you most likely to do? I recall one student telling me that he improved his golf game simply by choosing to focus on landing the ball on the green rather than not putting it in the water. Remember, what you focus on is what you get!

What is your usual response to the question "How are you?" If you tend to reply with "Not bad," the next time you're asked this question, consider saying, *"Great!"* with matching voice tonality and physiology. Notice the effect this new response has on you as well as on the person who asked the question.

The use of negatives has its place and in some situations can be used to your advantage. Consider the following: as your employer, I am about to assign you a very difficult task. I could say either "This task will be difficult" or "I will not suggest to you that this task will be easy." Notice the different internal representations that each phrase generates. Which is more appealing to you? As we will see when we discuss the Milton model (hypnotic language patterns), often these negatively stated sentences include an embedded command. For example, "Don't *tell your friends how much you enjoyed this book.*"

Generally, state what you or others should do, not what not to do.

"And" is often better than "but"

You have just finished sharing an idea with a colleague and the first word out of her mouth is "but…." What's your reaction? Do you think she was actually listening? Do you feel she has rejected your idea? Now assume she said "and" instead of "but." Does this feel different? Do you have the feeling she was listening and is now building on your idea?

There are definitely times when the word *but* is useful. Yet far too often we use *but* when *and* is a better choice.

Be careful with the word "try"

How often do you hear or say, "I'll try"? And what does this mean? Sometimes the word "try" is used to mean "I really don't want to do what you have asked, and I don't know how to say no to you," or "I don't have sufficient confidence in myself to make a full commitment to getting this done," or "I don't know what I really want in life."

When I hear people express their dreams or outcomes with the word *try*, I usually ask myself, "How serious is this person about achieving their dreams?" What messages are you sending to your unconscious mind? I see this as having one foot on the playing field and the other foot in the stands and hoping to score a touchdown. Highly unlikely! Trying is a waste of energy. Other equally noncommittal words that we use are *want, hope* and *wish*.

> *Try*? There is no *try*. There is only *do* or *not do*.
> – Yoda, *Star Wars: The Empire Strikes Back*

Take a moment to review your "to do" list – the one you keep in your head or the one that you actually write down. Do you find the sheer number of items on your list overwhelming and demotivating? How many of the items fall under the category, "I will try to get this done"? What do you think is possible and how would you feel if, right now, you followed Yoda's advice and identified those that you are clearly prepared to do (and have the time and resources to do so), while removing the others from the list?

For each of your dreams, identify clearly what it is you want; define it in measurable terms with time frames and commit to doing it. For more information on this, see chapter 7.1 on outcome MASTERY.

As a coach, ask questions

We often find ourselves helping or coaching family members, friends, colleagues, staff or clients. The techniques and ideas in this book can help you individually as well as in a coaching role with others.

When working with clients, I prefer to ask questions rather than suggest to them what they should do. I believe that at some level of consciousness, we all know what we need to do to live our dreams; we just need someone to assist us in discovering what it is. If I tell you what *I* think you should do, my suggestion will be tainted with my model of the world, and I am encouraging you to be at effect rather than at cause. If I were to create a space for you to feel safe exploring your inner thoughts, and then ask you questions that assist you in discovering what is true for you, you would then be at cause for how your life unfolds.

Future pacing

Future pacing is often the last step in an NLP technique. Your client has gone through the NLP technique and made the changes that she desires. Now you ask your client to go out into the future, where a similar situation to the problem scenario may arise, and to describe how she feels or reacts given her new choices, knowledge and resources. Use your sensory acuity to notice any shifts that may indicate that your client is not fully congruent with these new choices or behavior. If your client is not fully congruent, additional work will be necessary.

Future pacing is a final test to verify that the changes have taken effect. It is also a mental rehearsal for your client. Mentally rehearsing the successful completion of a future situation significantly increases the possibility of success. You may want to do this several times – further convincing her that the change has been made.

A group of world-class Soviet athletes were divided into four subgroups. The first group spent one hundred percent of their training time in training. The second spent seventy-five percent of their time in training and twenty-five percent visualizing the exact movements and accomplishments they wanted to achieve in their sport. The third spent fifty percent of their time training and fifty percent visualizing, and the fourth spent twenty-five percent training and seventy-five percent visualizing. At the 1980 Winter Games, the fourth group showed the greatest improvement in performance, followed by groups three, two and one, in that order. (Charles A. Garfield, *Peak Performance: Mental Training Techniques of the World's Greatest Athletes* (New York: Warner Books, 1984), p.16.

Content free

Many of the NLP techniques are content free. That is, the client does not have to tell you his or her "story." Some understanding of your client's issue will help, but you do not need all the details. Some clients prefer not to reveal too many details, while others relish in telling the story. However, they may have told the story so many times that it has become a rote exercise; occasionally they may embellish in order to give it a little more zing. Having told their story so often, some clients may begin to accept this embellished story as reality.

Break state

For many of the NLP techniques, a critical step is involved that asks the client to *break state*. Quite simply, we want the client to clear her mind of the internal representations she was making and go to a neutral state. This is easily done by making a statement or asking a question such as the following: "Do you like my tie?" (Whether you are wearing a tie does not matter. Her looking to look to see whether you have a tie will clear her mind of the previous internal representations.) Other questions might be: "Do you like the color of this wall?" or "Oh, look the sun is shining." As well, you can ask your client to stand or to stretch (remember physiology affects internal representations).

Conscious and unconscious minds

George Miller, in his 1956 paper "The Magic Number Seven, Plus or Minus Two," from *The Psychological Review*, 1956, vol. 63, pp. 81–97, reasoned that the conscious mind is able to keep track of seven plus or minus two chunks of information at a time. Our unconscious mind, on the other hand, looks after all of our bodily functions and is the storehouse for all of our habits, decisions, beliefs, past memories and other information we have acquired.

You form habits by consciously learning several small chunks of information, and gradually combining these into increasing larger chunks until, at some point, they become a way of life and you simply do them unconsciously. This frees your conscious mind to become aware of other new information. Remember when you first learned how to drive a car? Where was your attention? Now you can drive a car, perhaps tend to your children or talk with your passengers in safety, since these behaviors are now unconscious or habitual.

To remember what you have learned, you can consciously call up several large chunks of information from your unconscious mind. Then, as you become more and more specific within each succeeding chunk size, you can request more specific information from your unconscious mind.

Our conscious and unconscious minds have distinct and mutually supportive roles. Sometimes, these two minds come into conflict, causing a lack of congruence within ourselves that is expressed in our behaviors. Parts integration (chapter 6.6) is very useful in resolving this type of conflict.

Why NLP techniques may not work

There are a number of reasons why NLP techniques do not work. The three most important reasons are:

- The client does not feel safe. The coach or therapist has either not established rapport and a feeling of trust with the client, has not adequately explained the technique and approach that she will be using, or the environment is perceived by the client as unsafe. If the client does not feel safe, he may go through the motions, but will not step into the unknown and make the changes he desires.

- Secondary gain. A client will manifest certain detrimental behaviors because, in his model of the world, he sees some benefit. From the perspective of an outsider, this so-called benefit may seem harmful, silly or irrelevant. What is important is how the client perceives his reality, not another person's perception of what it may be. If this secondary gain is not addressed or satisfied in some other manner, the client will eventually revert to his old behaviors to get this benefit.

When I first started using NLP, I helped a teenager who had a fear of snakes. His fear was such that if he knew a book contained a picture of a snake, he would avoid touching the book in any way. I used an NLP phobia cure and after ten minutes, the young man felt very comfortable holding books containing pictures of snakes and even touching these pictures. I future-paced possible situations where he might encounter a snake; he was also very comfortable with this. I did not, however, have a snake available to test that the phobia was indeed gone. If I had, I believe that he may not have wanted to touch the snake, but that he would have been comfortable in its presence and reacted in a rational manner, rather than his former, irrational behavior.

A month later, I found out that the snake phobia had returned. Upon further investigation, I discovered that his mother and father were separated, that he did not enjoy going to his father's cottage, and that there were snakes at his father's cottage. Instead of having the confidence to tell his father that he did not want to visit the cottage, the boy found that the snake phobia served a very useful function by giving him permission not to go. His phobia provided a secondary gain.

- Desired change is not in alignment with the higher logical levels (see section 3.6 Logical levels: The hidden traits that drive us). The logical levels are: spirituality, identity, beliefs/values, capabilities/strategies, behavior and environment. For instance, let's say the client wishes to change behavior involving giving oral presentations to groups. At present he has a deeply rooted belief that he is not good enough or that people in the audience know more about the subject than he does. If he fails to address the higher-level belief issues, any behavioral change he makes will eventually be over-ridden by these deep-rooted beliefs.

A word of caution

For the aspiring coach or the new student, NLP techniques can be very powerful. However, the true power comes from the proficiency of the person using them. Just as a world-class racecar driver can do things with her car that you and I can only dream about and should not attempt, so it is with the NLP techniques. I recommend that you practice these techniques in a safe environment, such as under the guidance of a fully qualified professional. Taking an NLP seminar is a good way to begin.

Cars bring a measure of value (and some detrimental effects) to each of us and our society. A car in the hands of someone who does not follow the rules of the road nor considers the safety and well-being of others is a serious problem and a threat to others. But it is not the car that is at fault; rather, the person who is using the car inappropriately. So too with NLP. Please use the power of NLP techniques with integrity and, if in doubt, seek the advice of qualified professionals.

3.

Getting to Know Yourself and Others

3.1. MODALITIES AND REPRESENTATIONAL SYSTEMS

There are five primary sensory modalities that we use to experience the world around us (the *neuro* of neuro-linguistic programming). These are the visual (V), auditory (A), kinesthetic (K), gustatory (G) and olfactory (O). Kinesthetic can be external – tactile sensations like touch, temperature and moisture, or internal – remembered sensations, emotions and inner feelings of balance and body awareness. These modalities are also known as *representational systems* (or rep systems); they are the primary ways we represent, code, store and give meaning or language (the *linguistic* of NLP) to our experiences.

In NLP, we often work with three representational systems: visual, auditory and kinesthetic. Although primary senses, the gustatory and olfactory do not play a major role and are often included with kinesthetic. However, if you or your client is a chef, works with fragrances, or is a person who uses and relies on your gustatory or olfactory senses to a large degree, these senses need to be considered separate from kinesthetic. Many NLP practitioners split the auditory system into two components: auditory tonal (A_t – sound) and auditory digital (A_d – words as discrete verbal symbols or digits). As you will see in later chapters, we also make a distinction between the internal and external modalities. For example, if I am looking at my car, this is the visual external modality, indicated as V^e. On the other hand, if I am seeing my car as an image in my mind only, this is classified as visual internal, indicated as V^i.

We can access more than one representational system at the same time, for example, listening to music (A_t^e) while seeing a picture of a friend in the mind's eye (V^i). As we will discover when we cover strategies, our behavior is produced from a mixture of internal and external sensory experiences.

Preferred representational systems

We use all of our senses and, at any given time, depending upon the circumstances, may focus on one or more of them. When listening to a favorite piece of music, for instance, we may close our eyes to more fully listen and to experience certain deeper feelings.

Each of us has preferred representational systems. For example, when learning something new, some of us may prefer to see it or imagine it performed, others need to hear how to do it, others need to get a feeling for it, and yet others have to make sense of it. In general, one system is not better than another. However, depending on the context, one or more of the representational systems may be more effective. Landscape painters will tend to use visual modalities; musicians, auditory tonal; athletes, kinesthetic; and mathematicians, auditory digital. People at the top of their profession typically have the ability to use all of the representational systems and to choose the one most appropriate for the situation.

Depending on your preferred representational system(s), you may exhibit certain behaviors or characteristics. Before exploring these behaviors, please note that, depending on what is going on in your life – the context – you may change your preferred representational system(s) from time to time. Hence, as a coach, it is more useful to notice the representational system a person is currently favoring, rather than pigeon-holing him or her.

The following are generalizations of the characteristics of people with a preference for visual, auditory tonal, kinesthetic or auditory digital. Remember, as with all generalizations, there are always exceptions.

Visual
People with a visual preference will tend to:

- Be organized, neat and well-groomed. Why? Because they want to *look* good. And what do they expect from you? Yes, the same thing.
- Use *visualization* for memory and decision-making – often getting *insights* about something.
- Be more *imaginative* and may have difficulty putting their ideas in words.
- Speak faster than the general population. Why? Because they have a *picture(s)* in their mind and, if it is a moving *picture*, there is much to tell in a relatively short time.
- Prefer in-person interactions – to *see* the other person and his or her reactions.
- Want to *see* or be *shown* concepts, ideas or how something is done.
- Want to *see* the big *picture*.
- May not remember what others have said, and become confused if they

are given too many verbal instructions. However, if you can draw a *map* or *picture* for them, they can *see* what you are saying.
- Remember faces more easily than names.
- Be distracted by *visual* activity and less so by noise.

Auditory Tonal
People with an auditory tonal preference will tend to:

- Be more aware of subtle change in the *tone* of your *voice* and be more responsive to certain *tones* of *voice*.
- Perceive and represent sequences and are able to remember directions or instructions more easily.
- Learn by *listening* and *asking* questions.
- Enjoy *discussions* and prefer to communicate through *spoken* language rather than the written word.
- *Talk* through problems and like to have someone available to serve as a *sounding* board for their ideas.
- Need to be *heard*.
- Be easily distracted by *noise*.

Kinesthetic
People with a kinesthetic preference will tend to:

- Speak slower than the average person. Why? Because they need time to get in *touch* with how they *feel* about the topic.
- Be more sensitive to their *bodies* and their *feelings* and respond to *physical* rewards and *touching*.
- Learn by *doing*, *moving* or *touching*.
- Dress and groom themselves for *comfort* rather than for appearance.
- Make decisions based on their *feelings*.
- Stand closer to other people than those with a visual preference in order to *feel* the other person's *energy*, whereas the person with a visual preference will stand back to observe more of the other person's body language.

Auditory Digital
The auditory digital modality is devoid of the physical senses. People with an auditory digital preference will tend to:

- Have a need to make *sense* of the world, to *figure* things out, to *understand* concepts.
- Talk to themselves and carry on conversations with you in their mind. They may say they recall discussing something with you, when the conversation actually never took place. However, to the A_d person, a mental conversation with you is very real.
- Learn by working things out in their minds.

- Not be spontaneous, as they like to *think* things through.
- Have *logic, facts* and *figures* play a key role in the *decision*-making process.
- Memorize by *steps, procedures* and *sequences*.

I have a PhD in statistics. Does this give you some idea as to my preferred representational system, at least when I was working on my PhD? Remember, I may have changed my preferences over time. If you said auditory digital (facts and figures, logic), you are partially correct. I also had a preference for visual, although this modality was weaker than auditory digital; I was able to visualize mathematical formulations in my mind and work them through before committing them to paper. Many scientists and inventors have a highly developed ability to visualize.

Can you see yourself in one or more of these representational systems, does one sound better than the others, do you feel one is a better fit than another, or is one more logical? In Appendix A, a small preference test is presented to help you decide which is (are) your preferred representational system(s).

3.2. PREDICATES AND LEAD REPRESENTATIONAL SYSTEMS

Predicates

What do you notice about the following four sentences?

- You have shown me a bright idea on how to proceed and I'd like to look into it further.
- You have told me of a way to proceed that sounds great and I'd like to hear more about it.
- You have handed me a way to proceed that feels very good and I'd like to get more of a handle on it.
- You have provided me with a way to proceed that makes good sense and I'd like have more details.

The first sentence uses visual words, the second auditory, the third kinesthetic and the fourth uses words that are not sensory based (auditory digital), yet all four sentences convey the same general meaning.

You use words to describe your thoughts. If your thoughts – your internal representations – are mainly pictures, then you will tend to use more visual words when describing your thoughts. If the basis of your thoughts is logic or making sense of something, you may use words that reflect the logic of your thinking. Likewise for auditory and kinesthetic. The words you use reflect your internal thought processes. This is a very important point to be aware of as you convey your internal thoughts and thought structures to others through the words you choose to use or not use.

In NLP terms, visual, auditory, kinesthetic and auditory digital words and phrases are called *predicates*. The predicates a person uses will provide you with an indication of that person's preferred representational system.

The following table lists some of the different NLP predicates and predicate phrases. This is not a complete list. Can you think of other words or phrases that might be added? Notice that some words like *fuzzy* can appear in more than one column.

Visual	Auditory	Kinesthetic	Auditory Digital
see	hear	grasp	sense
look	tell	feel	experience
bright	sound	hard	understand
clear	resonate	unfeeling	change
picture	listen	concrete	perceive
foggy	silence	scrape	question
view	deaf	solid	sensitive
focused	squeak	fuzzy	distinct
fuzzy	hush	get hold of	conceive
dawn	roar	catch on	know
reveal	melody	tap into	think
illuminate	make music	heated argument	learn
imagine	harmonize	pull some strings	process
hazy	tune in/out	sharp as a tack	decide
an eyeful	rings a bell	smooth operator	motivate
short-sighted	quiet as a mouse	make contact	consider
bright outlook	voiced an opinion	throw out	describe in detail
take a peek	clear as a bell	firm foundation	figure it out
tunnel vision	music to my ears	get a handle on	make sense of
bird's eye view	loud and clear	get in touch with	pay attention to
naked eye	purrs like a kitten	hand in hand	word for word
paint a picture	on another note	hang in there	without a doubt

You use visual, auditory, kinesthetic and auditory digital predicates all the time. Some contexts imply the use of only one type of predicate; for example, if I asked you to describe a picture on your television, you would most likely use visual predicates. And finally, if there is a choice, you will tend to use the predicates from your preferred representational system.

Sometimes we don't speak the same language

Have you ever explained something to someone, who responded with, "I don't see what you are saying" or "I can't picture this." What is at work here? One possibility is that the person is highly visual. You, however, have been using words other than visual; hence, your listener is having difficulty forming a picture of your explanation in his or her mind. And how do we usually handle this situation? We repeat the same words over again, only this time with emphasis, as if our listener had heard nothing the first time around!

Given what you have learned thus far about NLP, how can you approach this situation differently so your listener can *see* what you are saying? One possibility is to use visual words to help her form a picture in her mind, or you may wish to draw a diagram or picture.

Of course, it is not just visual people who may have difficulty with your explanation. An auditory person may say, "This doesn't sound right." A kinesthetic person may say, "I don't have a feeling for this." An auditory digital person, "This does not make sense."

If you pay attention to the words people are using, you'll find they are revealing to you how they see, hear, get in touch with or make sense of the world around them.

Relationships and representational systems

Think about a time when you first started dating someone. You probably made certain you looked good by dressing and grooming appropriately; you took your date places to see attractions; you used appropriate voice tonalities and enjoyed the music; you touched and held hands; you made sure that you smelled good and visited different restaurants to taste different foods. In other words, you used all the representational systems to suitably impress and charm your date.

At some point, two people move beyond the "dating" stage and become a couple or perhaps get married. And often, instead of using all the representational systems or sensory modalities, they will revert to those they prefer. If one member of the couple is visual, she will want to get dressed up to go out and see a show, and expect and give gifts that are visually appealing – including the wrapping. If he, on the other hand, is kinesthetic, he will want to dress comfortably, touching and holding hands, and giving and receiving gifts that exude a feeling. If these two people do not learn to express their individual needs and expectations in terms of their preferred representational systems, as well as showing flexibility in satisfying those of their partner, they each may be in for a difficult ride. Has this happened to you?

Exercise 1:
For two minutes, describe your home using only visual words. Repeat this exercise for two minutes each, use only auditory words, followed by kinesthetic words and, for the final two minutes, only auditory digital words. Hint: for visual, you can describe the different colors; for auditory, the different sounds; for kinesthetic, different feelings or textures; and for auditory digital, you can use facts and figures. Notice which modality (or modalities) gives you the most difficulty. These are the ones you will need to practice. If you want people to clearly see, hear, grasp and understand your message, you need to be able to speak their language.

Exercise 2:
Listen to the predicates that your friends or family members use. They will use a mixture of visual, auditory, kinesthetic and auditory digital predicates and one or two of these will be used more frequently. This is their preferred representational system.

Rapport with others is very important. One way to increase your rapport with another person is to match the predicates they use. That is, if they use mainly kinesthetic words in their speech, then you should use more kinesthetic words when speaking to them.

Lead representational systems

As you've learned, people have a preferred representational system – some have more than one – for their conscious thinking. In order to bring something to your conscious awareness, you use a *lead* representational system. You also use the lead representational system to initiate the input of information into your memory. Your lead representational system may be the same as your preferred representational system, or it may not.

For example, let us say my preferred representational system is visual. If someone asks me about my last vacation, I may first get in touch with all the good feelings about my vacation before fully bringing up the pictures in my mind. In this case, kinesthetic is my lead representational system: it leads the way for the visual.

Lead representational systems may vary depending on contexts. For example, before accessing the feelings associated with a very distressing event, I may choose to first access the event through pictures and thus slowly ease myself into the feelings associated with the event.

Overlap and synesthesia

Overlap

As we go through life, it is natural for us to create a link or *overlap* between two or more senses. Hearing a particular song or gentle tone of voice may produce romantic feelings; you may see different colors in your mind as a piece of music is played; looking over the edge of a cliff or tall building may generate a panic response. This overlapping of senses provides richer and more memorable experiences.

Overlapping senses can also be used purposefully to enhance an event. A motivational speaker may use lively music with bright visual displays and lighting effects to create a powerful and moving motivational effect. On the other hand, if you wanted to create a relaxed, peaceful atmosphere, you could combine slow soft music with video of a gently flowing stream in a tranquil country setting.

Many NLP techniques use overlap:

- As a coach, you can use overlap to assist a client in accessing a less frequently used representational system. Your client may say that he cannot visualize, yet has no problem accessing feelings or sounds in his mind. If your client enjoys going to the beach, have him remember what it feels like to walk across a cool sandy beach in his bare feet, feeling the warm sun on his body and the gentle breeze on his face. As he gets into these feelings, begin to introduce sounds, such as the sound of the waves on the beach and seagulls in the distance. Now begin to intersperse visual sights in between the kinesthetic and auditory cues and have him notice that he does indeed have visual memories of this experience. Continue to repeat this type of exercise until he can easily visualize different events.

- To create a *resource anchor* (see chapter 5.2) – a trigger that when fired puts you into a positive mental state – you are often asked to visualize how you would look and act with specific resources and then to notice how you would feel.

Synesthesia occurs when two or more senses are so overlapped that you have difficulty distinguishing one sense from another. A mixture of visual, auditory or kinesthetic predicates usually indicates a synesthesia: the beautiful flowers *caught* my eye, the music *feels* good, I *see* what you are saying, hearing his voice gives me a *bad taste in my mouth*. Examples of synesthesia include the warm or cool feeling you get from certain colors, or when you see or hear something that causes a noticeable feeling in the pit of your stomach.

Overlaps and synesthesias generally add to our enjoyment of life through creating more memorable and moving experiences. However, because the linkage of the senses is so strong, synesthesias can be a significant component of a phobia or other debilitating problems. To address this type of problem, techniques such as *V-K dissociation* (chapter 6.7) and *timeline* (chapter 6.2), which unlink the senses, separate what you are seeing from what you are feeling.

3.3. EYE ACCESSING CUES

Have you ever noticed that people's eyes move when they are thinking? This is valuable information that can provide you with clues as to whether they are thinking in pictures, sounds, feelings or talking to themselves. It is information about their lead and preferred representational systems.

William James, in his *Principles of Psychology* (1890), first suggested that internal representations and eye movements might be related. This observation was not explored further until the 1970s, when Richard Bandler, John Grinder, Robert Dilts and others conducted further experimentation in this area.

According to neurological research (Ehrlichman, H., & Weinberger, A. (1978) "Lateral eye movements and hemispheric asymmetry: A critical review." *Psychological Bulletin,* 86, 1080–1101.), eye movement both laterally and vertically seems to be associated with activating different parts of the brain. In the neurological literature, these movements are called lateral eye movements (LEM), and in NLP, we call them *eye accessing cues* because they give us insights into how people are accessing information.

To understand how your eyes move, consider the following questions. For each question, as you think of the answer, notice the direction(s) your eyes move – up, down or to the side. Or, if your eyes do not seem to move, notice whether you have a sense that you are looking in a certain direction, even if only for a fraction of a second.

- What is the color of your front door? *visual, up*
- What will you look like in fifteen years?
- What does your favorite music sound like? *auditory, lateral*
- What would your voice sound like if you had marbles in your mouth?
- When you talk to yourself, what type of voice do you use? *kinesthetic, down*
- What does it feel like to be in a nice, warm bath?

Did you notice your eyes had a tendency to look up for the first two questions, to the side for the next two questions and down for the last two questions? In general, if you are forming a picture in your mind, your eyes will tend to go up to the left or the right; for sounds laterally to the left or right; and down to the left or right for feelings or when you talk to yourself.

More specifically, if you are right-handed, you may have noticed the following (for people who are left-handed, exchange left and right in the following text):

- Question 1 – eyes up and to your left. This is a question about something you have seen before; hence, you remembered it – visual remembered (V^R).
- Question 2 – eyes up and to your right. This is a question about something that I assume you have not seen before; hence, you constructed this picture – visual constructed (V^C).
- Question 3 – eyes on the horizontal plane to your left. This is a question about something you have heard before – auditory remembered (A^R).
- Question 4 – eyes on the horizontal plane to your right. This is a question about something you have not heard before – auditory constructed (A^C).
- Question 5 – eyes down and to the left. This is a question about your self talk – auditory digital (A_d).
- Question 6 – eyes down and to the right. This is a question about your feelings – kinesthetic (K).

Note: The above eye patterns are how *your* eyes would move if you are right-handed. The following picture describes the eye patterns for a right-handed person as *you look at him or her* – please note this distinction. These patterns are fairly consistent across all races. For many left-handed people, the chart is reversed (a mirror image).

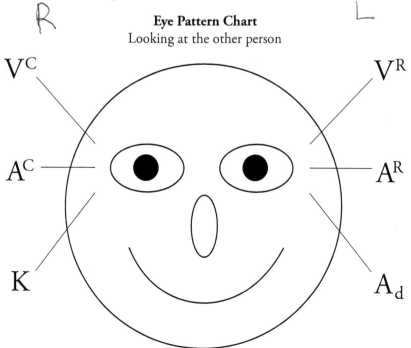

Eye Pattern Chart
Looking at the other person

If you would like to have some fun with your friends or family, here are some other questions you can take turns asking one another – or you can make up your own.

Visual remembered
- What is the color of the shirt you wore yesterday?
- Which of your friends has the shortest hair?

Visual constructed
- What would your room look like if it were painted yellow with big purple circles?
- Imagine the top half of a tiger on the bottom half of an elephant.

Auditory remembered
- What does your best friend's voice sound like?
- Which is louder, your doorbell or your telephone?

Auditory constructed
- What will your voice sound like in ten years?
- What would it sound like if you played your two favorite pieces of music at the same time?

Auditory digital
- What is something you continually tell yourself?
- What are your thoughts about this book?

Kinesthetic
- What does it feel like to walk barefoot on a cool sandy beach?
- What does it feel like when you rub your fingers on sandpaper?

People's eyes do not always move
Sometimes people's eyes do not move. This may be due to:

- The "look-to-talk" rule. That is, when you are making eye contact with some people, they will return your gaze directly, and their eyes will seem not to move, or move only very slightly and quickly. In this situation, they may be defocusing their eyes so their "internal" eye can look in the appropriate direction.
- Near-term memory. If the answer is something that is well-known to the person (i.e., their own name) or is a recent observation, they will not need to search their minds for the answer and their eyes will not move.

Using eye patterns to assess congruence
If a person is describing something they have seen or heard, their eyes should primarily move to visual or auditory remembered. However, if a person is inventing something or telling a lie, their eyes will tend to move to visual or auditory

constructed, indicating they are constructing some part of the situation being described. This may indicate that the person is uncertain or untruthful about what they are thinking.

Be careful in assuming someone is untruthful. For example, suppose you ask me a question about something I had never thought about before. To formulate an answer, I may have to look at or hear one or more pieces of true information in a way I have never done before. In this situation, I would be constructing an answer and my eyes would most likely move to visual or auditory constructed.

Lead and preferred representational systems

People's eye movements relate to their lead and preferred representational systems. For instance, I am right-handed and my lead system is auditory digital. If you were to ask me to recall the color of my front door, my eyes would first go down to my left (auditory digital) before going up to my left (visual remembered). Why? Because the first thing I would do is repeat the question and make sense of it (auditory digital), and then formulate the answer (visual remembered).

In a similar manner, if your lead system is visual, and I asked you what it feels like to be in a nice, warm bath, you would likely form a picture of being in the bath (visual remembered) before accessing the feeling itself.

Remember, the preferred representational system is the sensory modality – visual, auditory, kinesthetic or auditory digital – a person uses to organize and understand some experience or situation. If I am speaking to someone or giving a presentation and I notice that their eyes keep going up to visual, even if I am not using visual words or pictures, this is a clue that they may be forming visual internal representations; therefore, their preferred representational system is visual. To assist them in creating this picture in their mind, I should use more visual words in my presentation. On the other hand, if their eyes are tracking on the horizontal plane, this means they are processing in sounds, and their preferred representational system is auditory. If their eyes move downward, they may be processing kinesthetically or attempting to make logical sense of what I am saying (auditory digital). If, in addition, their eyes move downward to the right and they are right-handed, their preferred representational system is most likely kinesthetic.

Transderivational search

Did that long word capture your attention? *Transderivational search* means that a person's eyes are moving to all six areas as they seek the answer. If you see this happening, it means they are going deep in their memories to find an answer. Give them a moment to think. Avoid disturbing them by offering more information or asking more questions. If you speak while a person is making eye movements, you will interrupt their thinking.

A thought for teachers

Some teachers expect a student to look at them when asked a question. If, in response to a question from the teacher, little Johnny looks up to "see" the answer, the teacher may respond with, "The answer is not on the ceiling, so look at me." In this situation, little Johnny may not be able to answer the teacher, because he is not able to look up to "see" the answer.

Strategy elicitation

Eye accessing cues give you insight into a person's thought processes and their strategies – strategies for decision-making, career choices, falling in love, motivation and learning.

Why would you want to know a person's strategy? There are two main reasons why this is useful. First, if they are exceptionally good at what they do, it would be useful to know how they do it so you can replicate the process for yourself and others. Second, if they have come to you for advice or coaching about something that is not working in their life, it would be helpful to understand the process or strategy they are using. Armed with this understanding, you are in a position to help them design a different, improved process that leads to the outcomes they desire.

If you are interested in a person's decision-making strategy, you may wish to ask them to recall the last time they made an important decision and what steps or method they used to reach that decision. If they respond with uncertainty, it may be because the answer is outside of their conscious awareness. However, the sequence of eye accessing cues may reveal the basic steps (three to five). For example, their eyes may move to auditory remember, then to visual constructed, then to auditory digital and finally to kinesthetic. Put another way, their strategy may have the following basic building blocks: First, hear something about the decision to be made; next, visually construct possible alternatives or see what may happen as a result of the decision; and finally, make sense of what they know and feel good about the decision they are about to make.

Strategy elicitation is discussed in more detail in chapter 5.5.

Building your confidence in reading eye accessing cues

There are a number of ways to practice reading eye accessing cues. Here are two:

- With their permission, practice with your friends. Watch their eye accessing cues and then verify your observations with them.

- Watch talk shows on TV (be sure the show is spontaneous and not rehearsed). This is a great way to practice – you can stare at the people on the TV and it will not bother them at all. Notice whether there is a relationship between where the person looks and the predicates they use. For instance, if the person's eyes are looking up, do they tend to use more visual words?

3.4. SENSORY ACUITY

Are you consciously aware of what is going on around you or inside of you? Are you just going through the motions of living? Are you responding to the opportunities that are there – if you just take a moment to choose to see, hear, feel or experience them? Are you listening to your internal signals when it comes to taking action, or are you doing what you think others expect or demand of you? Perhaps it is time to begin paying attention to these signals.

Sensory acuity – seeing, hearing, feeling (physically and emotionally), smelling and tasting – is a critical piece of NLP and your life. It is important for you to be aware of:

- Feedback/information that indicates the extent to which you are on or off target in achieving your outcomes.
- Other people's actions and reactions to certain situations/stimuli.
- How you are reacting to certain situations/stimuli.

Achieving your outcomes

The five steps for success detailed in chapter 2.4 emphasize the importance of having an outcome for whatever you do. This is the first step for success. The third step, after taking action, is to pay attention and have some form of measure to know whether you are making progress toward your outcome. What are the signs (visual, auditory, kinesthetic, olfactory or gustatory) that indicate whether you are on course? If you are not, what corrective action is required? If you do not use your sensory acuity, you may end up far off course or spend more effort than is required.

For example, have you ever encountered a salesperson who has the sale in hand but doesn't realize it – she continues talking and eventually talks her prospect out of the sale? Or have you ever discovered after the fact that you did not pay attention to what was important to a loved one, and you ended up missing a great opportunity for communication? Or perhaps you failed to heed warning signs at work and missed a potential opportunity during a reorganization.

Often we pay attention through our preferred representational system and miss subtle – or even obvious – changes available through the other representational systems. These may manifest in another person as a change in tone of voice or skin color or demeanor, and may be critical for achieving our outcomes or avoiding problems.

Observing other people's actions and reactions

Whether you are coaching another person, delivering training to a class, negotiating with another person or sharing an intimate moment with a loved one, it is important to understand how people experience the world around them. You need to recognize their preferred representational systems in order to more clearly express your ideas so they can see, or hear or get in touch with your message. You should also be perceptive of changes in another other person's physiology, tone of voice and energy that may indicate a change in their internal thoughts or emotional state. If this is the case, you may need to stop what you are doing and alter your approach. Yet how often do we miss these signals and continue doing what we have always done, somehow expecting different results the next time.

When observing other people, you will want to notice:

- Words they use (predicates).
- Eye movements (eye accessing cues).
- Changes in skin color and tone.
- Breathing.
- Voice quality and tone.
- Posture and gestures.
- Changes in energy – many people with kinesthetic as a preferred representational system or who are visually impaired are very attuned to changes in energy. We all have the ability to do this; we simply have not taken the time to practice the skill.

Pay attention to your internal and external signals

Often we do not pay attention to what is going on inside ourselves. How often have you had an instinctive reaction that said, "No, don't do this!" or "Yes, this is what I really want to do!" but you ignored it and later regretted your action or inaction. For some of us, the internal signals or physiological reactions are present, but we are just not aware of them – perhaps because we have ignored them for such a long time that they are now out of our conscious awareness.

Some of the internal or physiological responses to which you could start paying attention are:

- Holding your breath. Do you hold your breath when you are stressed? When you hold your breath, your body does not get enough oxygen, which causes even more stress. When you notice you are holding your breath, take this as a signal to give yourself permission to breathe deeply at a relaxed pace.

- A tightening in your stomach or chest.
- A certain pain or twitch.
- A feeling of joy, love or accomplishment – or are these the feelings you tend to ignore?
- Internal representations (images and sounds) you create in your mind.

I believe it is very important for me to be aware of what is going on inside of me. There are only two conversations in this world. The first is the one I have with myself and the second is the one that I have with you. If I do not feel resourceful or good about myself, this will be evident in my conversation with you through my choice of words, my tone of voice, my body language and the energy emanating from me. Even if you are not consciously aware of these signals coming from me, you will sense them at an unconscious level and react to them in some way.

> What's going on in the inside shows on the outside.
> – *Earl Nightingale*

Practice your sensory acuity

This exercise is a two-person exercise – let's call them Bill and Irene. Irene's job is simply to observe Bill.

1. Bill closes his eyes and thinks of someone he dislikes.

2. While Bill thinks about this person, he begins at the top of his head and slowly moves his attention down his own body, noticing any physiological reaction to thinking about this person. For instance, he may notice tension around his eyes, a pain in his shoulder or a heavy feeling in his stomach. As he is scanning his body, he tells Irene what he is observing.

3. Once Bill has finished describing what he has observed, Irene tells Bill what she has observed. For example, she may have observed his eyes closed tightly, a red flushing around his neck, very shallow breathing, twitching of a finger on his right hand, a certain tone of voice or an energy pushing her away from him.

4. Once step three is completed, Bill stretches and/or looks around the room – a break state – and clears his mind of the internal representations of the person he dislikes.

5. Bill closes his eyes and repeats steps two and three while thinking of someone he likes.

6. Again, create a break state by stretching or looking around the room.

7. Bill may find he is surprised at the different internal and external reactions he had between thinking of some he dislikes and someone he likes. He may also be surprised by the reactions that he was not aware of – those that Irene described to him. As a result of this exercise, Bill may discover that he really does telegraph his feelings and thoughts to others, even if it is at an unconscious level.

8. Bill chooses one of the two people he had been thinking about earlier, and does not tell Irene which person it is. He closes his eyes again and thinks of this person.

9. From what she had observed earlier, Irene tells Bill who he is thinking about. Almost like magic!

A caution

For sensory acuity, we must stick with what we have seen, heard, felt, tasted or smelled. We should not project an opinion or guess. For example, you may observe that my lips curl up at the ends in the form of smile, which is a fact. You may then tell me that I am happy, which is a guess, a hallucination or a mind read. The smile may be a result of the fact that I have any number of things taking place mentally or physiologically.

Mind-reading has the potential to get us into trouble. Consider someone who is angry versus someone who is very determined and focused on completing a task. The external physiological cues may be quite similar. If we ask the determined person why he is angry, he may indeed get angry with us for making an erroneous judgment about him.

3.5. META PROGRAMS

Meta programs are filters that determine how you perceive the world around you. They have a major influence on how you communicate with others and the behaviors you manifest.

Meta means *over, beyond, above*, or on a *different level*. These terms all suggest you are operating at an unconscious level. Meta programs are deeply rooted mental programs that automatically filter our experiences and guide and direct our thought processes, resulting in significant differences in behavior from person to person. They define typical patterns in the strategies or thinking styles of an individual, group, company or culture.

Leslie Cameron-Bandler originally identified about sixty different patterns. Fortunately, subsequent researchers have combined many of these together to form a much smaller and more useful set. The number and descriptions of the patterns vary slightly from author to author. In this book, we have chosen to work with the meta programs as described by Rodger Bailey. Bailey describes two types of meta programs – *motivation traits* and *working traits* – and has adapted them for use in business settings. They are equally effective in non-business situations. Bailey determined that people who have the same language profile generally have the same behavior patterns. Hence, on the basis of the words a person uses, we can make predictions about his or her behavior. Also, once we have determined a person's behavior patterns, we can choose specific words that will have the most influence on that person. Bailey refers to this as the *language and behavior profile*, or *LAB profile*. (Reference: Shelle Rose Charvet, *Words that Change Minds: Mastering the Language of Influence*, Kendal Hunt, 1997)

Some points to consider

- Meta programs may vary across contexts. Those may include your work or home environments, and they may change over time as you learn new information or experience significant events in your life.

- If you have difficulty imagining or relating to someone who lives their life in the way the following meta programs suggest, you are probably at the other end of the spectrum. On the other hand, if you relate entirely to one of these descriptions, then this is most likely true for you. And of course, you may be in the middle, between the two extremes.

- For each meta program, it is important to realize that where you are positioned is how you live your own life, and that other people may see the world quite differently. If you wish to have a meaningful conversation or relationship with people who have different meta programs, you need to respect their model of the world, be flexible and speak to them in their language.

- You can identify a person's meta programs from the language they use as well as their behaviors.

- As managers, we tend to hire people who are like us – those who have similar meta programs – and form teams of "like" people. However, often teams and business units function most optimally if they comprise people with different viewpoints, motivation and work traits.

As you read the following meta programs, you are encouraged to identify your preferences and notice what you are creating as a result of these choices. For example, the first meta program is Toward – Away From. Toward people are focused on what they want to achieve. They may harbor this trait to the degree that they do not see problems lurking just below the surface – problems that can get them into trouble. While they can benefit from the help of an Away From person, this is the very type whom they will tend to avoid, because the Away From person is always telling them what may go wrong without allowing them to fully express their ideas.

On the other hand, a person who is highly Away From often sees only what may go wrong in a given situation. This can be annoying to others who feel a need to move forward. If you are an Away From person, the problem may be that you interject too quickly: others feel that you have not allowed them time to express their ideas. You may wish to listen more to others' ideas and, when they are finished, ask them whether you can identify a few areas that may give them trouble. In either case, you may benefit from a strategy used by Walt Disney that acknowledged and provided time for both of these points of view to be considered. This strategy is covered in chapter 5.5.

Motivation traits

1. Toward – Away From
Is the person motivated by goals and achievements or by issues and problems to be resolved or avoided?

Toward: These people are focused on their goals. They are motivated to have, achieve and attain. They tend to be good at managing priorities but sometimes have trouble recognizing what should be avoided or identifying problems. They are clear in terms of what they want. To motivate or influence these people, use words such as accomplish, attain, get, achieve, rewards, goals. To identify this type of person, notice whether they use these words themselves, and whether they speak about achieving goals and outcomes. An ideal type of job for this person would be one that is outcome oriented. These people would make poor proofreaders, as they are not looking for mistakes.

Away From: People in this group notice what should be eliminated, avoided or repaired. They are motivated when there is a problem to be solved or trouble in need of fixing. They are good at troubleshooting, solving problems and pinpointing possible obstacles because they automatically see what is wrong. They may set goals; however, they will abandon them immediately if there is a pressing problem. They have difficulty managing priorities. You can motivate or identify this type of person with the following words and phrases: avoid, steer clear of, prevent, eliminate, solve, get rid of, fix, prohibit. An ideal career would be one that involves identifying problems – proofreading or quality assurance managing. Their management style is crisis management.

Distribution in a work context: Toward – 40%, Toward and Away From – 20%, Away From – 40%.

2. Internal – External

Does the person assess their performance through their own internal standards and beliefs or through information and feedback from external sources?

Internal: These people have their own internal standards and make their own judgments about the quality of their work. They have difficulty accepting other people's opinions and outside direction. If they receive negative feedback regarding something they believe they have done well, they will question the judgment of the person giving the feedback. As a result, they may be difficult to supervise. They assess information from outside sources according to their own internal standards. Since they do not need feedback on their own progress, as managers, they tend not to give feedback to others. You can motivate this type of person with the following phrases: you know what's best, only you can decide, it is up to you, I need your opinion. Their ideal job is one in which they can make their own decisions.

External: People in this group need to receive outside direction and feedback to stay motivated and to know how well they are doing. Without external validation, they may feel lost or have difficulty starting or continuing an activity. They may interpret a simple discussion as an order and then feel overwhelmed with all you have directed them to do. They are motivated by phrases such as: according to the experts, others will think highly of you, you will be recognized for your efforts. These people make good customer service representatives.

To identify whether a person is Internal or External, ask them a question such as, "How do you know you have done a good job?"

Distribution in a work context: Internal – 40%, Internal and External – 20%, External – 40%.

3. Options – Procedures

Does the person prefer to keep their options open and explore alternatives or feel most comfortable following established procedures?

Options: People in this group are motivated by the possibility of doing something in alternative way. They are the type of people who will develop procedures and not follow them. They enjoy breaking or bending the rules. Exploring new ideas and possibilities is of great interest. They may begin a new project and not feel compelled to finish it. To motivate or influence these people, use words and phrases such as: alternatives, break the rules, flexibility, unlimited possibilities, expand your choices, options. Listen for these words to help you identify this type of person. These people do well in situations that require solutions or alternatives to current systems – fashion designing, process re-engineering.

Procedures: These people like to follow established rules and processes. Once they understand a procedure, they will follow it repeatedly. They have great difficulty developing new processes and feel lost without a clearly defined procedure. They are more concerned about how to do something than about why they should do it. Bending or breaking rules is sacrilege! They are motivated by words and phrases such as: correct way, tried and true, first/then, lastly, proven path. Positions suited to these people would be bookkeeping or commercial airline piloting.

Distribution in a work context: Options – 40%, Options and Procedures – 20%, Procedures – 40%.

4. Proactive – Reactive
Does the person tend to initiate or prefer to wait for others to lead?

Proactive: People in this group tend to initiate and not wait for others. From a reactive's point of view, they act with little or no consideration, jump into situations without thinking or analyzing and bulldoze ahead with their own agenda. They excel at getting the job done. To motivate or influence these people, use phrases such as: go for it, just do it, why wait, take charge, what are you waiting for. To identify these people, notice whether they use short sentences with an active verb, speak as if they are in control or have difficulty sitting still for long periods of time. These people do well in situations where something needs to be done now – outside sales, project management (when getting the job done is more important than the "feathers that may get ruffled").

Reactive: These people have a tendency to wait for others to initiate or until the situation is right. They may spend substantial time considering and analyzing without acting. They want to fully understand and assess before acting; they also believe in chance or luck. They are motivated by phrases such as: consider the following, let's investigate this further, analyze this, we need to understand this, this time we will be lucky. This group can be identified through their use of long complex sentences or incomplete sentences, use of passive verbs and nominalizations (verbs transformed into nouns, i.e., communication rather than communicate), use of conditionals (would, should, could, might, may). They will also speak in terms of outside forces having a major influence on their lives and relying on luck or the need to understand and analyze before acting. Positions suited to these people would be analysts or customer service representatives.

Distribution in a work context: Proactive –15 to 20%, Proactive and Reactive – 60 to 65%, Reactive – 15 to 20%.

5. Sameness – Difference
Does a person look for things that are the same or different?

Sameness: People in this group want their world to remain the same. They may accept change every ten years and will instigate change only every fifteen to twenty-five years. To motivate these people, point out how things have not changed, that they are still doing the same type of work. Use phrases such as: same as, similar to, in common, as you always do, like before. They are best suited to work environments that do not change or change very slowly over time.

Sameness with Exception: These people like to see change happen slowly over time. They look for significant change every five to seven years. Words and phrases that motivate these people are: improved, better, more/less, same except, gradual improvement.

Difference: Change is a way of life for people in this group. They expect or will orchestrate major change every one to two years. Motivating words include: new, fresh, totally different, completely changed, radical idea. If you are looking for radical change in your organization, these are the people who will lead it, and, of course, they are the people who will demand it.

Sameness with Exception and Difference: People in this group expect major change every three to four years. They thrive on a balance between steady progress and major upheaval. Motivating words and phrases would include a combination of those used for the sameness with exception and difference groups.

How to identify the different groups: You could ask the following question: "What is the relationship between your work (or home, or vacation) this year and last year?" Listen for the words listed above. Even if they have changed jobs during the past year, Sameness people may talk about what the two positions have in common, and how things really have not changed. Sameness with Exception people will talk about how things are evolving or about similarities first and then differences, while Difference people may not understand the word "relationship," because to their thinking, there is no relationship between what they are doing now and what they did last year. Sameness with Exception and Difference people will have a blend of the responses of these two types.

Distribution in a work context: Sameness – 5%, Sameness with Exception – 65%, Difference – 20%, Sameness and Difference with Exception – 10%.

Motivation traits – concluding thought
We have discussed each of the traits separately. To get greater insight, look at various combinations. For example, what would most likely be the meta programs for an entrepreneur? I suggest: toward, internal, options, proactive and difference. Rodger Bailey talks about a highly successful entrepreneur with the

following pattern: toward, external, options, proactive and difference. This person compensated for his lack of internal referencing by hiring a business coach from whom he could obtain the necessary external feedback.

Working traits

6. Specific – General
Does the person prefer to work with details or the big picture?

Specific: People in this group prefer to work with small pieces of information and many details and facts. They see information in linear sequences and may have difficulty drawing it together to form an overview or big picture. They can be identified through speech patterns that have a definite sequence and contain much detail (adverbs, adjectives, proper names of people, places and things). Motivating language includes providing lots of detail in a clearly defined sequence and using words such as: exactly, in particular, specifically. These people make good assembly line workers and bookkeepers, as they enjoy working with details for long periods.

General: People in this group prefer to work at the theoretical, abstract or big picture level. If necessary, they can work at the detail level but will become bored or frustrated quickly. Their thoughts may seem disconnected as they describe various aspects of the big picture, which they see in its entirety. When they speak, they may provide an overview or present abstract concepts in simple sentences with few modifiers or details. To motivate these people, you need to avoid details, describe the big picture and look for generalizations. They are good at planning and developing strategies and make good project managers.

Distribution in a work context: Specific – 40%, Specific and General – 20%, General – 40%.

7. Self – Others
Is the person focused on his or her own internal experience or on the non-verbal behavior of others?

Self: People in this group focus on themselves and do not tend to show emotions, although they do have them. They are more focused on the content of a conversation rather than the non-verbal communication – body language or tone of voice – and have difficulty establishing and maintaining rapport. They are not skilled at interpersonal communication; they assess the quality of the communication on their own feelings and not other people's reactions. To identify these people, notice whether they react to the content of the conversation rather than your body language or tone of voice. As well, they will show little facial expression or voice variation. If you accidentally dropped a pencil or book, they would tend to ignore it and expect you to pick it up. To influence these people, focus on the content of your message. These people are best suited for technical positions where their interaction with other people is not critical to effective, productive work.

Others: These people pay attention to others and tend to be more animated, responding to the body language and tone of voice of the other person. They assess a conversation at a conscious or unconscious level based on their observations of the other person. They tend to be good at establishing and maintaining rapport. These people can be identified from their animated behaviors, body language and changes in voice tonality to match the content of their communication. If you accidentally dropped a pencil or book, their natural tendency is to pick it up for you. They are most influenced by the depth of rapport established. These people make good customer service representatives.

Distribution in a work context: Self – 7%, Others – 93%.

8. Independent – Proximity – Co-operative
Does the person prefer working alone, with people close by or as part of a team?

Independent: These people prefer to work alone and have sole responsibility for getting the job done. If they work with others or share responsibility, their productivity may decrease. They prefer to work in isolation and do not readily consult with other people. If you ask these people about a particularly enjoyable work experience, they will talk about their own accomplishments and not mention others playing a role in completing the task. To influence these people, give them total responsibility and make it clear that they alone will work on this task. These people are most productive when they work independently, even if the work environment around them is chaotic.

Proximity: People in this group enjoy having clearly defined responsibilities and being in charge. They need others to be involved, without sharing responsibility or control. If you ask these people about a particularly enjoyable work experience, they will talk about what they did and suggest that other people assisted in getting it done. To motivate these people, put them in charge and provide them with subordinate staff to direct. This is a good attribute (with some co-operative skills) for managers.

Co-operative: These people enjoy working with others in a team environment, where responsibilities and control are shared, and everyone takes turns leading. If you ask these people about a particularly enjoyable work experience, they will talk in terms of "we," "us," "our team," and that the responsibility and accomplishments are a result of everyone's contribution. To motivate these people, talk about shared responsibility, "we are all in this together," and use the words *we* and *us*. These people are ideally suited to a team environment that requires sharing of responsibilities and work tasks.

Distribution in a work context: Independent – 20%, Proximity – 60%, Co-operative – 20%.

9. Feeling – Thinking – Choice

Is the person highly emotional, or does he or she tend to stay calm or show a balance of the two?

Feeling: These people react emotionally to normal levels of stress and tend to have difficulty getting out of the emotion. Highly stressful jobs are not suited to them and others may view them as overreacting. To identify members of this group, notice whether they tend to have an emotional response when describing a difficult situation, and take some time to recover. To motivate these people, focus on the emotional aspect of the task and use words such as: passionate, exhilarating, extraordinary. Artistic careers would be most suited to these people.

Thinking: Thinking people remain calm in stressful situations, may have trouble empathizing with others and have difficulty establishing rapport. To identify this group, ask them about a particularly stressful situation and notice that they describe it without emotion. Cold hard facts logically presented without emotional content will motivate this group. A position such as an air traffic controller is ideally suited to people with these traits.

Choice: People in this group can easily be emotional about a stressful event and just as easily come out of the emotion. They are able to choose how they react. To motivate this group use a mixture of emotional words together with logical facts. They make good managers as they are able to empathize and maintain a distance, depending on what is called for.

Distribution in a work context: Feeling – 15%, Thinking – 15%, Choice – 70%.

10. Thing – Person

Does the person focus on inanimate and intangible objects (ideas, systems, gadgets) or on feelings and thoughts?

Thing: For this group, everything is a thing – systems, work activities, people and ideas. They want to get things done and believe work is no place for emotions. They speak mostly about inanimate things and people are simply part of a larger process. To motivate these people, use impersonal pronouns, talk about systems and objectives with a focus to getting the job done. Ideal jobs involve working with systems or in a role where the personal touch is not required.

Person: Feelings are very important to members of this group and can become the main focus. They establish rapport with others very easily. This group talks about people and their feelings and uses personal pronouns and the names of other people. To influence these people, speak about feelings, use people's names, make it feel like they are in one big happy family. Customer service is an area suited to these people.

Distribution in a work context: Thing – 55%, Thing and Person – 30%, Person – 15%.

Shelle Rose Charvet, in her book *Words That Change Minds: Mastering the Language of Influence* (Kendall/Hunt Publishing Company, 1997), describes the above meta programs in more detail, presents three other meta programs and discusses how meta programs can be used for hiring, team building, organizational change, sales, marketing and negotiation.

3.6. LOGICAL LEVELS: THE HIDDEN TRAITS THAT DRIVE US

The NLP logical levels (also known as the logical levels of change and the logical levels of thinking) are very useful for assisting with or understanding change from an individual, social or organizational point of view. They were developed by Robert Dilts and are based on the "neurological levels" proposed by anthropologist Gregory Batson. (Robert Dilts, *Changing Belief Systems with NLP*, Meta Publications, 1990). The six logical levels, their hierarchy and the questions that assist in defining these levels are presented in the table on the following page.

We operate at all of these levels. Depending on the circumstances, some levels are more important than others. If I am crossing a very busy street, it is very important that I pay attention to the Environment and Behavior levels – where I am and what I am doing.

An example:
To gain an appreciation of how these logical levels work, here is an example. Assume it is 9:00 a.m. and I am at my place of work (environment).

If I don't want to be there, then I must change my behavior. I have several possible choices: I could walk out. I could do cartwheels over to and out the door. I could start yelling and screaming, with the hope someone would take me out of the building.

The behavior I select depends on my capabilities and strategies. If I am capable of performing cartwheels, then this is certainly a possibility. On the other hand, my strategy may be to have someone help me to leave; I could begin yelling and screaming to effect this. Or, if I really don't want to work there and need some source of income, my strategy might be to become ill so that I have a medical excuse and can go on long-term disability. Do you know anyone who has done this – either consciously or unconsciously?

LOGICAL LEVELS	
Level	**Questions corresponding to logical levels** (for individuals or organizations)
Spirituality/ Purpose	**Who else?** This can be viewed as your connection to a larger system or a higher power. If you are an individual or company providing NLP-related services, what impact are you having within your community (where you live and work, the NLP community), your culture and the culture of others?
Identity/ Mission	**Who?** Who are you as an individual or company? What role does the organization fulfill? What role do you play to achieve your purpose? How do you think of yourself? For example, I am a successful person.
Beliefs/ Values	**Why?** Why do you do something? What do you believe in or value? As an individual, you may believe you can do anything you choose. Or you may value honesty. From a company perspective, the company may value good customer service and/or the well-being of staff.
Capabilities/ Strategies	**How?** How do you go about doing things? As an individual or company, what are your capabilities, skills, strategies or action plans?
Behavior	**What?** What are your behaviors? What does the organization do?
Environment	**Where? When? With whom?** Where, when and with whom do you display your behaviors? What are the external influences and constraints upon you or the organization?

The capability or strategy I choose will depend on my beliefs and values. If I believe that I can easily get another job to support my family, then becoming ill is not a choice for me.

My beliefs and values are determined by my identity. If I see myself as a successful person, then it is very possible that I would hold the belief that I can easily get another job or even create a business of my own.

My identity is dependent on my purpose in life – the impact that I wish to have on my friends, family, community and society.

Sustainable Change

The above example illustrates that a logical level has significant influence over those levels below it and little influence over those levels above it. Thus, for personal or organizational change to be long-lasting and sustainable, the change must either be in alignment with the higher logical levels or must be effected at the highest possible logical level.

Using logical levels to explain/understand change

The above examination of logical levels leads to a number of interesting observations:

1. Short-term versus long-term change: Some people have found that NLP techniques worked effectively at changing an unwanted behavior for a short period, but eventually the unwanted behavior returned. How can this be? Simply put, if the new behavior was not in alignment with the person's beliefs and values or identity, the higher level would eventually override the lower level.

    As noted above, for change at the behavior level to be long-term, the desired behavior change must either be in alignment with the higher levels or the change must take place at a higher level.

2. Organizational change: Have you ever been involved in change within an organization? What are some of the more common change activities?

    How about a new organization chart? Or perhaps a change in the physical layout of the offices. This is change at the level of environment. Do you think it will be long-lasting? Only if the change is in alignment with the higher logical levels.

    Or perhaps staff are informed they must perform in a different way behaviorally, without receiving the necessary training – capability/strategy. Unfortunately, this happens far too often. When corporate finances become tight, often the first thing cut is the training budget. Again, the change will most likely not be long-lasting, because the behavioral level is not supported at the capabilities/strategies level.

On the other hand, people in an organization will change their behaviors if the change provides them with something they perceive to be valuable. Unfortunately, many organizational change initiatives explain the change only in terms of how it will help the company and, by association, the employee rather than in terms of direct value for the employee.

3. Health: Suppose your outcome is to live a healthy lifestyle, a behavior level activity. Further, suppose you see yourself as a successful businessperson and you value success far more than health. Do you think you will achieve your outcome?

4. I have heard many people refer to the following quote by Albert Einstein:

> The problems of today can only be solved at a higher
> level of thinking than that which created them.

And I have met few people who can explain how this is actually achieved, that is, how it is possible to move to that higher level of thinking. Using logical levels, it is easily explained. If there is a problem at the behavioral level, for example, to solve it you must move to at least the capability/strategy level.

Getting to know another person

Suppose a spaceship landed in your town. What do you know about it? Do you know its purpose? Its mission? Its beliefs and values? Its strategy? No, not without contacting it, establishing trust and safety, a means of communication, and asking meaningful questions; all you know is what it is doing (behavior) and when and where and with whom (environment) it is doing it.

It is the same when you are interacting with another person. If you do not establish trust and safety and ask meaningful questions at the higher logical levels, you will never truly get to know that person. In fact, many people have never asked *themselves* these very questions; thus they amble through life aimlessly without being consciously aware of their beliefs and values, identity or purpose in life.

Having conversations with another person at the higher logical levels provides you with a more intimate understanding of that person and why they behave in the manner they do. How often do you have a conversation with someone you really care about, yet the topic does not go beyond the weather (environment) or what they are doing (behavior)? To discover the true essence of this person, you instead need to be discussing who they see themselves being (identity/mission) or what is important to them about life, career or relationships (values).

To engage in this type of conversation, you need to create a space where each of you feels safe in disclosing your "inner selves."

Teaching/training

A number of years ago, I was an associate professor of statistics at the University of New Brunswick. The faculty of nursing required all of its students to take a statistics course in the first term of their last year. Over the years, this course had developed a bad reputation, mainly because it was taught by professors who approached it as a mathematics class. As you might have expected, most of the nursing students had difficulty with the course. Every year, there would be a lineup of students outside the dean's office complaining about the course and asking for help.

Then it was my turn to teach this class! I will explain how I changed the nature of the subject matter to appeal to the students. Before proceeding, let's examine this situation through the lens of the logical levels.

Nursing students' general characteristics:

Spirituality/purpose (connection to a larger system): To make a significant contribution to the community of people who require medical assistance, support or compassion.

Identity/mission: To become highly trained medical professionals who can assist people in their time of need.

Beliefs/values: Value helping others and believe they have or will acquire the necessary nursing skills and the innate compassionate nature required to assist others together with a belief that they can successfully undertake activities related to nursing. Another important belief held by many of the nursing students was that they could not comprehend mathematics. (Before the class began, a number of nursing students met with me, expressing concern for the class and their incomprehension with mathematics, a subject they had dropped in high school.)

Capabilities/strategies: Many positive capabilities/strategies for nursing. Less than supportive (in some cases dysfunctional) capabilities/strategies for mathematics.

Behavior: The behaviors of a competent medical professional when working in a nursing environment. Distressed behaviors when asked to perform in a "mathematics environment" – in some cases, almost paralyzed with inaction or breaking into tears.

Environment: A nursing environment or a mathematics environment.

At the time, I did not know about logical levels; however, I did know that I had to take a new approach in delivering this course. I first spent some time researching in the university library. Instead of using dry statistical exercises that were far removed from nursing, I was determined to appeal to the students from their perspective of the world. In the medical journals, I was able to find many medical examples that used statistics. I used these examples for classroom discussion and homework exercises. In effect, I changed the course from a statistics course to a nursing course, and both the students and I ended up enjoying ourselves immensely. In the second term, as part of their honors project, a number of the nursing students undertook projects that had a significant statistical component – a community health survey of the province of New Brunswick.

From a logical levels point of view, can you see why my approach was successful and that of the other professors was not?

Might you use a similar approach with your family, staff or colleagues that would allow them to see the situation differently and to draw on their strengths to overcome a perceived obstacle?

Aligning logical levels for personal congruence

In NLP, when we talk about personal congruence, we often mean an internal alignment among the logical levels just discussed. For many of us, the logical levels operate outside of our conscious awareness. Whether we are aware of them or not, they have a significant influence over the quality of our lives.

The following exercise will help you to: 1) Become consciously aware of which factors influence how you live your life. 2) Identify possible conflicts. 3) Recognize possible changes you can make to bring the levels more in alignment and hence achieve a higher level of personal congruence (reduced inner conflict). First identify a context or larger system, for example, your family, work, community, or people in need of a particular service or product. Next, answer the following questions. Some people find it easier to begin with Environment and work their way up. This is fine, as long as the last pass goes from Spirituality to Environment.

Spirituality/purpose: For the larger system, what is your purpose or the impact you wish to have?

Identity/mission: Who are you or what role do you play? Does the role fully contribute to achieving your purpose? What do you need to change in order to fully achieve your purpose?

Beliefs/values: What beliefs do you have about yourself, about others, about the world in general? Do these beliefs support you in fulfilling your role? What do you value – in yourself, others, the world in general? Are these values in alignment with your role? Are there other beliefs and values you could take on that would be more in alignment?

Capabilities/strategies: What capabilities/strategies/action plans do you have? Do you need to develop new capabilities, strategies or action plans? Are they in alignment with each of the above logical levels? If not, what needs to be changed? Perhaps you need to change your capabilities (get more training), your strategies or action plans. Or perhaps, given this new information, you need to reassess your purpose, your role or your beliefs and values.

Behaviors: What do people really see or experience in your behaviors? Are your behaviors in alignment with each of the above logical levels? Does something need to be changed?

Environment: When, where, with whom do you exhibit these behaviors? Are they in alignment with the above logical levels?

Using logical levels for organizational restructuring

A few years ago, I was called upon to help a client who had recently been appointed to head a new group composed of two units that had operated separately in the past and now were expected to operate as one under my client.

Before I was called in, representatives of the two units had met a number of times and not progressed in agreeing on how the two units should be merged. Any guesses why? As I discovered, the impasse occurred because the conversations took place at the Behavior and Environment levels only, without the benefit of a higher-level context, such as this unit's new role, or the larger community it was to serve. Nothing had been determined except that the two units would be merged.

My first step was to determine the new unit's connection to a larger system (spirituality/purpose) – to whom they were to provide a service or product, who was providing a service or product to them, and any other communities indirectly affecting them or affected by them. After this had been established, I formed a working group with representatives from these different groups as well as representatives – management, officers and support staff – from the two units that were to be merged.

In facilitated sessions, in the following order, we: 1) verified the larger system, 2) formulated the role (identity/mission) of the new unit, 3) decided on the beliefs and values required for this new role and verified with everyone around the table that they were acceptable, and 4) identified three key capabilities/

strategies that the new business unit needed to adopt. We stopped at this point as everyone in the working group realized that these three capabilities/strategies were precisely how the new business unit should be organized – three divisions, each responsible for one of the capabilities/strategies.

Two key points are worth mentioning:

- The three capabilities/strategies that the working group formulated were entirely unexpected and had not been discussed or raised at any time prior to our discussion on capabilities/strategies. However, they were obvious once we worked our way through the logical levels.

- There were representatives from suppliers, clients and members of the new unit.

  o As the issues of roles, beliefs, values, strategies and capabilities of the new unit were raised and discussed, people noted either how adopting a certain role, belief/value or strategy/capability would negatively affect their current business operations, or that they would be glad to realign their processes as it would save their business unit time or money. Taking this into account, the final set of recommendations was a win-win for all parties involved.

  o Members took the recommendations back to their respective communities, and, because the proposal met their current needs and was proposed by one of their own members, it received the necessary buy-in and support.

4.

Improving Your Communication

4.1. RAPPORT

Rapport is the foundation for any meaningful interaction between two or more people – whether it relates to sales, negotiation, providing information or directions to a co-worker, a conversation with a family member, during training or coaching, or in your personal relations. Rapport is critical for all you do in business, at home or at play.

Rapport can be described in a number of ways. For me, rapport is about establishing an environment of trust, understanding, respect and safety, which gives all people the freedom to fully express their ideas and concerns and know that these will be respected by the other person(s). Rapport creates the space for the person to feel listened to and heard; it does not, however, mean that one person must agree with what another says or does. Instead, each person appreciates the other's viewpoint and respects their model of the world.

When you are in rapport with another person, you have the opportunity to enter their world and see things from their perspective, appreciate why they feel the way they do, and arrive at a better understanding of who they are; as a result, the whole relationship is enhanced.

Consider the following:

- Have you noticed when people enjoy being with each other, they have a tendency to use the same words and phrases, dress in a similar way or have matching body language?

- Have you observed that people who are not in rapport have differing postures, gestures, voice tonality or don't make eye contact? Have you ever had an opportunity to observe someone who did not want to attend a meeting or who did not trust the other people at the meeting? Did you notice a difference in their body language, voice tonality and choice of words compared with others in the meeting?

- Next time you are in a restaurant, look around and you'll observe people who are enjoying each other's company exhibiting similar postures, gestures and voice tonality.

- Have you ever been a long way from home and met someone new, and through casual conversation discovered they are from your own hometown? Or perhaps you learn that you both attended the same university, or are both interested in the same sport, or both enjoy the same type of music. What happens? Before long, you are engaged in a very animated conversation, seeking even more common experiences.

- Have you ever gone to a party or event for which the dress was formal, yet someone arrived dressed very casually? What was your first reaction? Did you feel that they somehow did not belong to the group? Or have you been at a restaurant and everybody at your table has been served their food but you? How did you feel? Uncomfortable, out of place?

The above points illustrate:

- The more we like the other person, the more we want to be like them.
- The more we have in common with another person, the stronger the bond with them.

Establishing rapport by matching and mirroring

The key to establishing rapport is an ability to enter another person's world by assuming a similar state of mind. This is done by becoming more like the other person – by *matching* and *mirroring* their behaviors, including body language, experiences, verbal language and tone of voice. Matching and mirroring are powerful methods of developing an appreciation for how the other person is seeing and experiencing the world.

The terms matching and mirroring are used interchangeably by some NLP practitioners, while others draw the following distinction: When you mirror someone, it is as if you are looking into a mirror. To mirror a person who has raised his right hand, you would raise your left hand – a mirror image. To match this same person, you would also raise your right hand – doing exactly the same as this person. I do not draw a significant distinction between matching and mirroring and refer to both of them as matching.

Consider matching body language first, then voice and finally the person's words. Why? Mehrabian and Ferris ("Inference of Attitudes from Nonverbal Communication in Two Channels," *Journal of Counselling Psychology*, Vol. 31, 1967, pp. 248–52) discovered that fifty-five percent of the impact of a presentation is determined by your body language, thirty-eight percent by your voice and only seven percent by the content or words you use. The percentages will differ in different contexts; nonetheless, body language and voice tonality have a major impact on your communication and ability to establish rapport.

Body language includes body posture, facial expressions, hand gestures, breathing and eye contact. As a beginner, start by matching one specific behavior and once you are comfortable doing that, then match another and so on.

For voice, you can match tonality, speed, volume, rhythm and clarity of speech. All of us can vary aspects of our voice and have a range in which we feel comfortable doing so. If someone speaks much faster than you do and at a rate at which you would not feel comfortable, match this person by speaking a little faster, while staying within a range that is comfortable for you.

For spoken language, match predicates. If your partner is using mainly visual words, you should also use mainly visual words; likewise for auditory, kinesthetic and auditory digital words. To the extent possible, you should also use the same words as the other person. For example, I may say something is "awesome." In your model of the world, you may interpret "awesome" as "outstanding" and use this word when speaking to me. For me, "outstanding" may have a different meaning or evoke a feeling different from "awesome." In this case, you would not be matching but mismatching my words. If you have identified the other person's meta programs, you can use words that match those meta programs.

Some people find the idea of matching another person uncomfortable; they feel they are trying to fool or take advantage of the other person. To overcome this uneasiness, realize that matching is a natural part of the rapport-building process and that you actually do it unconsciously every day with your close family and friends. Each day, gradually increase your conscious use of matching at a pace that is comfortable and ethical for you. Matching done with integrity and respect creates positive feelings and responses for you and in others. Rapport is the ability to enter someone else's world, to make him feel you understand him, and that there is a strong connection between the two of you.

Crossover matching

Crossover matching happens when you identify a particular behaviour of the other person and match it with a corresponding but different movement. If a person's breathing pattern is too fast or slow for you to feel comfortable matching, you can match the same rhythm of breathing with a rocking motion of your body, or by moving your foot or finger at the same pace. Crossover matching is useful if you wish to establish rapport with someone who is in a very unresourceful state – perhaps depression – and you do not wish to take on that state. Remember from the NLP communication model that your physiology influences your state and hence your thoughts.

Mismatching

Mismatching is also a useful skill to master. Sometimes, you may be too deep in rapport with another person to make a decision without the other person overly influencing you. In this case, you need to break rapport in order to create some thinking space. To do this, you mismatch. This can be done in a variety of ways. You can break eye contact by looking at your watch or brushing an imaginary piece of fluff off your arm. If you are both sitting, you can stand up. You may choose to mismatch with your voice by speaking faster or louder, or you may mismatch predicates.

Practice

You may wish to start with family members and begin to match different aspects of their posture, gestures, voice and words. Have fun with it and observe whether they notice what you are doing. At work or socially, start by matching one specific behavior; once you are comfortable doing that, match another. For friends, notice how often you naturally match their postures, gestures, tone of voice or words. Matching comes naturally; what takes practice is learning how to do it with everyone, not just those with whom you're already in rapport. In time, you'll find matching will become automatic whenever you wish to deepen your rapport with someone.

Pacing and leading

Pacing is the process of establishing rapport through matching. Once rapport has been established, *leading* is the process of changing your physiology, tone of voice, or choice of words to cause the other person to favorably change either his physiology or state. For example, you may have witnessed two people in rapport, pacing their behaviors agreeably. Then, one person changes his body position (leading), followed a few minutes later by the other person changing to this same body position. Why would this be useful? Suppose you are dealing with a colleague who is upset. You can pace his behavior by matching body language, voice and words. Once you have established rapport, you can begin to lead him into a calmer, more relaxed state by gradually changing your physiology and voice tonality to that of a calm state. A caution: if a person is angry, match with an intensity less than their level, otherwise you may worsen the situation.

Milton Erickson, the famous hypnotherapist, would pace a person's current experience by describing what they are experiencing as he slowly led them deeper into trance.

Exercise

To experience the value of establishing rapport through matching, consider the following two-part exercise you can do with a friend. Let's call the two participants Bill and Irene.

Part 1. Select a topic on which each of you has a different opinion. As you discuss this topic, Bill matches the body language, voice and language of Irene. Do this for about five minutes and notice what happens during the course of the conversation. Often what will happen is that although Bill and Irene originally had a difference of opinion, as the exercise proceeds they begin to either explore areas of agreement or find that they have a much better appreciation of the other's point of view.

Part 2. Select a topic on which you both agree. As you discuss this topic, Irene mismatches the body language, voice and language of Bill. Do this for about five minutes and notice what happens during the course of the conversation. For this part of the exercise, it is not unusual for Bill to become frustrated with Irene and not wish to continue with the conversation, even though originally they both agreed on the topic.

4.2. PERCEPTUAL POSITIONS

Different perspectives of the world

Often, it is useful to assess an event or outcome from several different perspectives or positions:

- First position: experiencing the situation through your own eyes, ears and feelings. You think in terms of what is important to you, what you want to achieve.

- Second position: stepping into the shoes of the other person and experiencing (seeing, hearing and feeling) the situation as if you were that person. You think in terms of how this situation would appear or be interpreted by the other person, taking on his or her beliefs, values, attitudes and personal history to the best of your knowledge. You've heard the expression: "Before criticizing someone, walk a mile in their shoes."

- Third position: standing back from a situation and experiencing it as if you were a detached observer. In your mind, you are able to see and hear yourself and the other person(s), as if watching strangers on a TV show. You act as an independent, resourceful third person and observe the interaction – the sequence of words, gestures, and expressions that occur in the communication – free of evaluation or judgment. You think in terms of what opinion, observations or advice an independent, uninvolved person would provide.

- Fourth position: the perspective from the system of which you are a part – i.e., a team, family, work or community system. You explore how your actions have an impact on the larger system, and how in turn the system constrains what you perceive is possible – crucial for understanding the group dynamics and your role (i.e., leader) within the group. The fourth position is also about ecology, that is, about checking the impact that your decisions will have on other people who will be influenced by proposed changes.

John Grinder and Judith DeLozier (*Turtles All the Way Down*, Grinder and Associates, 1987) developed the first three positions, which they referred to as *perceptual positions*. Robert Dilts added the fourth position (Robert Dilts, "Fourth Position," *Article of the Month*, 1998, http://www.nlpu.com/Articles /artic21.htm, accessed August 22, 2005). Perceptual positions provide a balanced approach to thinking about an event or outcome. In situations where there is little or no understanding or progress, they can provide a way of developing new understandings and creating new choices. The ability to experience yourself from different perspectives is an essential part of any good relationship, be it with colleagues, family members, friends or a special loved one.

All four positions are of equal importance and it is useful, consciously or unconsciously, to cycle through them as we go about our daily activities. Sometimes, however, we remain stuck in one of these positions:

- Someone who lives his life in first position would tend to focus on his own needs rather than the needs of others – a "self-centered" attitude. Addicts tend to see the world from first position.
- Someone who lives her life primarily in second position is always thinking about the other person at the expense of her own needs. Co-dependents or enablers in a dysfunctional or addiction situation would fit this description.
- Someone who lives in third position is a disconnected observer of life, quite capable of giving himself or others advice, and never putting it into action for himself.
- Someone who lives in fourth position would see all of the group dynamics and may not be aware of life outside of the group. That is, she would only have an identity within the group.

Improving your communication

You can do the following exercise alone or have someone guide you through it. Think of a conversation, discussion or disagreement you had recently with another person that did not go as well as you had hoped, and the situation remains unresolved. For ease of discussion, I will assume the other person is a male.

1. Are you prepared to explore this situation to find other ways to handle it, should a similar situation occur in the future? This is an important question. If you are committed to holding the other person as wrong and not prepared to learn and develop knew ideas from this experience, then proceeding is not worth your time. Pick another situation. If, however, you are committed to resolving the situation by exploring other avenues, proceed as follows.

2. Make yourself comfortable. Close your eyes and in your mind go back to that event, looking through your own eyes, seeing what you saw, hearing what you heard and feeling what you felt (i.e., first position). Once you have done this, open your eyes, look around the room, stand or stretch your body to break state. The purpose of this step is to remind yourself of the event and what you experienced.

3. Make yourself comfortable, close your eyes and go back to the event. This time, put yourself into the other person's body (second position), taking on his physiology looking through his eyes, seeing what he saw, hearing what he heard. To the best of your ability, experience how he felt being in a conversation with the person who looks and acts like you. Does this give you some understanding of why he reacted the way he did? If you were to give the person that looks like you some advice, from this perspective, on how to handle the situation differently, what would that advice be? When you are ready, open your eyes and break state.

4. Make yourself comfortable, close your eyes and this time look at the event as if you were a fly on the wall (third position). Some distance in front of you, you can see two people, one of whom looks, behaves and sounds like you. From this other perspective, notice the facial expressions, body language, hand gestures, tone of voice and words that the person who looks and acts like you is using. Can you advise this person on how the situation might be handled differently and possibly achieve a different, more positive result? When you are ready, open your eyes and break state.

5. Make yourself comfortable, close your eyes and this time look at the event from a system perspective (fourth position). From this perspective, notice the impact of your actions on the larger system. Is this what you had

planned to achieve? What advice can you give to the person who looks and acts like you so that a different result may be achieved? When you are ready, open your eyes and break state.

6. Repeat steps two through six, using the new behaviors and resources you identified in steps three, four and five. Did you notice anything different this time?

I often use this exercise in public presentations. At one event, as I finished the exercise, a young lady quickly left the room. She returned about twenty minutes later and, at the next break, approached me and apologized for leaving the room the way she had. She explained that about two weeks earlier, she'd had a major fight with her roommate and long-time close friend that resulted in her moving out. The two of them had not spoken to each other since. Now, however, as a result of doing the exercise, she realized how she could have handled the situation differently and left the room to telephone her friend. After the positive outcome of this new conversation, she was planning to move back in with her friend and roommate that very evening.

Exercises with perceptual positions can be used to learn from an event in the past, an event in the present (to gain an appreciation of how you are doing and whether you should take corrective action) or for a future event (for example, to rehearse a presentation).

Aligning your actions with your outcome

We live and function in all sorts of systems. Sometimes we have noble outcomes for ourselves and the system, yet our behaviors are not in alignment with our outcomes and we end up creating something other than what we desire. The following exercise will help you to align your behaviors with your outcome. It should be done on a daily basis until your behaviors are in alignment with your outcome(s).

1. Identify a specific system, for example, your family, work, team or community. Identify key members (or groups) of the system (if the system is your work environment, this may include your boss, your colleagues, those who work for you as well as your clients). Identify the outcome(s) you wish to achieve and keep it/them in mind as you go through the following steps.

2. Review your day from first position, noticing what you see, hear and feel as you interact with key members of the system. Break state.

3. From second position, for each key member (one at a time and break state between each second position), notice how they perceive your behaviors. Is this what you had intended to achieve? Is it moving you closer to achieving your outcome?

4. From third position, observe the interaction between yourself and key members (one at a time). Do these observations suggest possible changes you could make in your behaviors? Break state.

5. From fourth position, notice the impact your actions have on the whole system. Now, fast forward one, five or ten years into the future and notice the potential future impact of your behaviors. Is this what you planned to achieve? Do these observations suggest possible changes in your behaviors?

6. Taking into account the information you obtained from steps three through five, are there changes you would like to make in your behaviors to achieve your outcome, or does your outcome need adjusting? If the answer is yes, make these changes and repeat steps two through six. Continue with the above steps until your behaviors are in alignment with your outcome(s).

4.3. CHUNKING

Have you ever:

- Been stuck in a negotiation or argument and not been able to find common areas of agreement?
- Felt overwhelmed with an activity?
- Wanted to get something done, but did not feel excited about it?
- Needed to quickly and easily think laterally? Thinking laterally means getting a different perspective on a problem or issue.

Chunking can help you move beyond these obstacles.

What is chunking?

In NLP, *chunking up* refers to moving to more general or abstract pieces of information. *Chunking down* means moving to more specific or detailed information.

To chunk up on a piece of information, use one or more of the following questions:

- What is this an example of?
- What is this a part of?
- What is the intention?
- For what purpose?

To illustrate the concept, let us begin with a library building. Examples of chunking up from library building would be:

- Buildings (a library building is an example of many kinds of buildings).
- A city block (the library building forms part of a city block).

- A city's library system.
- A system that provides a means for people to undertake research.

If we follow the path of a city block, we can then chunk up to a city, then to a province or state, then to a country, and so on.

To chunk down, use one or more of the following questions:

- What is an example of this?
- What is a component/part of this?
- What/who/where specifically?

Examples of chunking down or being more specific on a library building are:

- A library building in the city of Seattle.
- A library building built in the 1950s.
- The third floor of the library building.
- A specific window in the library building.
- A shelf of books in the library building.

If we follow the path of a shelf of books, we can continue chunking down – getting more specific – to NLP books, then books written by John Grinder, then a particular chapter, and so on.

The above are just a few examples. Depending on your particular focus or thought pattern, you may come up with many different examples. In a real situation, the path you follow will be determined by the context and your intention.

How and when can you use chunking?

As a coach or manager, this simple concept of chunking has many varied and useful applications:

- Meta model and Milton model. The meta model is an example of chunking down (who, what, where specifically) – you ask your client questions to get more specific details. The Milton model, which uses vague or abstract language, is an example of chunking up. These two models will be examined at further length in chapters 4.6 and 4.7.

- Logical levels. You can chunk up or down on the logical levels. For example, if your client is exhibiting a certain behavior, you may choose to become curious and ask yourself: What strategy is this an example of? What is his intention? (i.e., what value or belief is being satisfied). To chunk down on a specific behavior, you may become curious as to where, when or with whom it is exhibited (environment level). If you start with a belief, you may chunk up to explore who this person sees himself as being – his identity – or chunk down to identify specific strategies or behaviors.

- Negotiation and mediation. Chunking up and down is a very useful tool in negotiation or mediation. Far too often in negotiation, we continue to explore solutions at a level of thought at which we do not agree. The key is to chunk up until you and the other person agree and then to chunk back down to the details only as fast as you both maintain agreement. Often in negotiation, we assume that the other person wants what we want, and this may not be the case.

During one NLP practitioner training session, we had covered chunking; the following morning we were discussing what we had learned in the previous days and how the students could use it. One woman from out of town described how she had called her husband and asked him what he wanted to do upon her return. He immediately suggested, "Let's go to the cottage for the weekend." Having been away from home for over a week, she found she did not relish the idea of repacking immediately and going to the cottage. Recalling the chunking technique, she asked him in a supportive tone, "You would like to go to the cottage – for what purpose?" His answer was, "To spend time with you." This approach opened up many more options for her to pursue that would meet her husband's need to spend time with her and that would also be very acceptable to her. I don't remember what they decided to do, but I do recall that she was very pleased and said it avoided a possible troublesome argument.

- Creating a passion for your outcome. By chunking up and down, you can size your outcomes so they are manageable and so that you have excitement, motivation and passion for achieving them.

  o Overcoming a lack of interest. Why do we get bored? Often because what we are doing does not excite us. We are mired in the details. If you have an outcome and you are not excited about it, ask yourself the question, "What is the purpose of this outcome?" This is an example of chunking up. Get a bigger perspective or the big picture. Having an outcome and not knowing the larger purpose can be demotivating.

  o Sometimes we may feel overwhelmed. This can happen if the chunk size is too large. Here we need to chunk down and be more specific, focus more on the details or be more realistic. After all, how do you eat an elephant? One bite at a time! If you feel overwhelmed or do not know where to start when you think of your outcome, chunk down to identify specific and manageable tasks.

- Creating rapport and improving your communication with others. If the person with whom you are speaking is more comfortable with details and you would like him to gain an appreciation for the bigger picture, chunk down to his level of detail, matching his chunk size to establish rapport and to show him you understand his view. Then gradually increase the chunk size to assist him in gaining an understanding of the larger picture. In a similar manner, you can assist a "big picture" person in chunking down to identify the steps necessary to move toward his outcome.

- Thinking laterally. We are often encouraged to think laterally. This is not always easy to do, but it can be if we use chunking. To think laterally, first chunk up, then chunk down. For example, suppose you have to take a package to a particular destination and you do not wish to use your car. To identify alternatives, first chunk up, i.e., what is driving your car an example of? One possible chunk up is a mode of transportation. Next, by chunking down, you can easy identify many different modes of transportation that are on the same logical level as car – perhaps a bicycle, bus, train, airplane or walking. From that list, you can select the mode that best meets your other needs.

- Brainstorming. Similar to thinking laterally, the first step in a brainstorming session would be to chunk up and then from this perspective explore ideas that satisfy this larger outcome.

4.4. DEEP STRUCTURE AND SURFACE STRUCTURE

At a deep level of thought, a speaker has complete knowledge of what he wishes to communicate to someone else. This is called the *deep structure* and operates at an unconscious level. To be efficient in his communication, the speaker unconsciously deletes, generalizes, limits or distorts his inner thoughts based on his beliefs and values, memories, decisions, strategies and what he wants you to hear. *Surface structure* is whatever he communicates – verbally, written, voice tonality and body language – to other people or to himself (his internal dialogue). What is finally communicated – the surface structure – is only a small subset of the original thought; it may be ambiguous or confusing and lead to miscommunication.

To illustrate deep structure and surface structure and why it is important to be aware of the distinction, let's assume you are my business coach, and are relatively new at your work and not well trained. Before saying or writing a word and often in a blink of an eye, my inner thoughts – my deep structure – are unconsciously filtered through my model of the world (i.e., beliefs and values). I then say to you, "My boss doesn't appreciate what I do." This single statement reveals only the surface structure of my communication. You, as my business coach, take in my words and at a deep level of thought – your deep structure – filter what I have said through your beliefs and values, memories and decisions.

On this basis, you may then say (surface structure) something such as "I know exactly what you are saying; here is what you should do." Your advice may be most appropriate for you and most inappropriate for me, as you have no real understanding of my interpretation of "my boss doesn't appreciate what I do." As a result, this may lead us to an argument because I feel you do not understand me and are always telling me what to do. I may become more entrenched in continuing with my limiting beliefs and behaviors.

To be an effective coach, you need to become curious about what I have said and to ask questions in order for us both to gain a better appreciation of my deep structure. Once we each have this clarity, you are in a better position to provide advice. What often happens is that when I, as the client, finally become clear on the issue and how to resolve it, I no longer need your advice, but simply your continued support and curiosity. Essentially, as a coach, you need to help me discover, through proper questioning and use of language, the path from my surface structure to my deep structure.

4.5. LINGUISTIC PRESUPPOSITIONS

NLP has two types of presuppositions – *linguistic* and *epistemological*. Linguistic presuppositions, the topic of this section, describe the information or relationships that must be accepted as true for the listener to make sense of what is being said. Epistemological presuppositions, on the other hand, are fundamental beliefs, rules or principles that form the base of a system. For example, our mathematical systems are built on a basic set of rules. The NLP epistemological presuppositions can be viewed as a fundamental set of principles on how you may choose to conduct your life.

A linguistic presupposition is something that is overtly expressed in the body of the statement itself, which must be presupposed or accepted in order for the sentence or utterance to make sense. It is an inference that can be made from the structure of language that provides a path from the words expressed by someone (the surface structure) to what is actually going on inside the person (their inner feelings, thoughts, memories, beliefs and values, often at an unconscious level – the deep structure). Linguistic presuppositions allow for the internal universe of the speaker to be revealed, and thus presumed by the listener from the words that the person is using. The information a person reveals through speech is not necessarily accurate or correct but will nonetheless reveal what he holds to be true in his model of the world. As the listener gains an understanding of the internal representations of the speaker, she can use different sentence structures or a change in words to offer the original speaker alternative internal representations for consideration – thus potentially assisting the original speaker in expanding or loosening his model of the world.

Presuppositions or a mind read?

As the receiver of a communication, it is important to distinguish between what is presupposed in the communication and what you superimpose or assume based on your interpretation of the communication through your filters – your history, beliefs and values. How often have you been in a conversation with someone and made an assumption about what they were saying, only to find out that you had guessed wrong? These inferences, deductions or conjectures that we create on the basis of how we see the world are called *mind reads*.

For example, consider the following sentence: "Ivan left town yesterday after causing a great deal of suffering." Which of the following are presuppositions and which are mind reads?

- There is a person called Ivan.
- Ivan will return and cause more suffering.
- Ivan physically hurt someone.

I was being tricky here – they are all mind reads! Ivan could be many different things – a person, a dog or a hurricane. There is nothing in the sentence that presupposes that Ivan will return. Ivan caused suffering, but we do not know if it was physical or emotional suffering. Did you identify them all as mind reads or did you make assumptions based on your model of the world?

More examples:
Read the following sentence and then decide what is presupposed: "My spouse's parents treat my children differently because they are handicapped." I have a spouse – yes; my spouse has parents – yes; I have children – yes; my children are treated differently – yes; my children are handicapped – mind read. It may be my spouse's parents that are handicapped.

Consider the following: "My life is a mess." Does this presuppose that the speaker has an understanding of what her life would be like if it were not a mess? Yes. You can only know whether something is hot if you have an understanding of what not hot (cold) is like. Instead of imposing your model of not mess on the speaker, you need to become curious and discover what she means internally by a mess and how, from her perspective, her life could be different.

Now consider the sentence, "I can't fix the problem." Assuming the speaker does not know how to fix the problem is a mind read. It is possible that the speaker does know how to fix the problem but is not able to do it now, possibly due to time restrictions or limited financial resources.

When you read the following, what do you think of? "When did your children first beat you?" Did you think of beating in the context of physical violence or in the competitive sense of winning at a sport or game, or something else? These are mind reads. From the information provided, you cannot know what "beat" means.

You will discover how to gain more clarity on what a person has said through the meta model, discussed at greater length in chapter 4.6.

Using linguistic presuppositions

You can use linguistic presuppositions to assist your listener in gaining a different perspective on a problem or the world in general. You also need to be aware of the presuppositions that you use in everyday language; they can have a significant impact on the listener. For example, after my father recently passed away, many well-intentioned people said things like: "I know you are sad at the loss of your father." To make sense of this sentence, I had to accept the speaker's presupposition of "being sad." What do you think was the potential impact on my emotional state? Now consider the sentence: "I know you will find the strength to cope with the loss of your father." Would this not put me in a different state of mind?

To gain a better perspective on the power of linguistic presuppositions, consider the following examples:

1. "Do you want to address your problem today or during our next session?" The main presupposition, or what the listener must accept to make sense of the sentence, is that "he will address the problem." In reality, he has many more options from which to choose. However, if he accepts the presuppositions in the sentence, his choices are limited to "today" or "during our next session." This is called a *double bind*.

   I have used double binds a number of times, with great results. In one situation, I was dealing with a large national company and getting the runaround from their staff. Fortunately, I had documented all of our communications. Finally, I wrote a letter to each member of the company's board of directors, with an attachment providing full details concerning how I had been treated. The final sentence of my letter was the following: "Either you fully support how your staff has handled this or you commit to resolving it in a way that is mutually satisfactory to all parties." (Notice the double bind.) Two weeks later, I received an offer that exceeded my expectations!

2. "Don't resolve this problem too fast." A presupposition is that it is possible to resolve the problem and the only real question is the speed at which it will be resolved.

3. "After you have finished this exercise, you will notice how easy it is to make the changes you desire in your life." Two possible presuppositions are: 1) the exercise will be finished, and 2) it is easy to make changes.

4. "Since you have volunteered for this exercise, you are making the changes now." Presupposes that the listener is already in the process of making the changes – whatever they may be.

5. "What issue do you want to address today?" This question is simple, direct and focuses the listener's attention on the fact that he will address an issue today.

6. Compare the following two sentences: "Are you continuing to improve your relationship with your family?" and "Are you improving your relationship with your family?" The word *continuing* in the first sentence implies that the listener has already been improving his relationship, while the second sentence has no such implication.

For linguistic presuppositions to be effective, they must be accepted by the listener's unconscious mind. Obviously, rapport and the listener having a sense of safety are essential to this activity, as is the case for any change-related activity.

Identifying and constructing presuppositions

The following structures will assist you in identifying or constructing linguistic presuppositions.

1. **Existence:** Suggests that something exists or *is*.

   "The boy moved to the front of the room." This presupposes the existence of a boy, a room, a front to the room and a back to the room.

2. **Possibility:** That something *can/can't* take place.

   "You can do anything you want to do." "You can resolve this when you choose."

3. **Cause–effect:** Indicates a sequencing of events; implies the flow of time, i.e., first one thing happens, followed by another as a direct result. Effect follows cause. Sentence structure may also include: If/when x happens, y follows, or y happened because x took place.

   "If you open the door, the cat can get out."

4. **Complex equivalence:** This phrase attributes meaning to something that may or may not have a "cause" capability. Implies both events are happening simultaneously.

"Reading this sentence means you are developing mastery." "Going to class means that I am a good student."

5. **Awareness:** Perception through one or more of the senses, either external or internal.

"Ron realizes that change is easy." To make sense of what Ron realizes, you have to accept the presupposition that *change is easy*.

6. **Time:** Indicators of past, present or future.

"I remember when I had problems." Indicates a present awareness of a past experience.

When working with a client, be aware of your use of time. Consider the following: "I understand you feel nervous when your boss calls you." "I understand you have felt nervous when your boss called you." Notice the second sentence presupposes that the problem is in the past.

7. **Adverb/Adjective:** Indicates degrees of relevance or intensity.

"This is a small problem." versus "This is a huge problem."

8. **Or:** Includes some things and excludes others. Reveals the presence of a double bind and an underlying assumption of the existence of something.

"Will you be finished today or tomorrow?" "I can travel by plane or by car."

9. **Ordinal:** Reference to numbers, sequence or frequency.

"The first thing to do is stop." Implies the possibility of subsequent actions.

Intonation patterns

Body language and intonation patterns are also part of the surface structure and imply (presuppose) information or relationships.

There are three intonation patterns: a statement, a command and a question. With a statement intonation, the voice tonality remains constant; with a command intonation, the voice tone lowers at the end of a sentence or ends emphatically; and with a question tonality, the voice tone rises at the end of a sentence.

Sometimes we use an inappropriate tonality. Suppose you have just assisted a client in resolving an issue and you say the following in a questioning tonality: "The process worked?" This would lead your client to doubt the efficacy of the process and wonder whether the issue was really resolved.

You can use intonation patterns to your advantage by asking a question with a command tonality. For example, "Are you willing to resolve this!" Given that you say this with a command tonality and that the last two words are an embedded command, the presupposition is set up for your client to resolve it.

4.6. META MODEL

The *meta model* provides us – as coaches, managers, therapists, family members and friends – with a set of questions to assist the person we are helping in moving from the surface structure of his communication to an understanding of his deep structure – his unconscious beliefs, values and decisions. The meta model is used to gather additional information and offers the potential of clarifying meanings, identifying limitations and opening up choices. An appropriate question asked with rapport can assist a client in exploring other possibilities and interpretations, with the potential to change his life. This is not about finding the right answers but about aiding you and your client in gaining a better understanding of his model of the world.

Origin of the meta model

John Grinder and Richard Bandler developed the meta model by modeling two very successful therapists, Fritz Perls (Gestalt therapy) and Virginia Satir (family therapy). These experts obtained extraordinary results from their clients by having them be more specific in what they expressed. That is, by using certain types of questions to gather information, they thereby gained an understanding of the client's deep structure. Grinder and Bandler observed that in moving from the deep structure to the surface structure, people unconsciously:

- Delete: We present only partial information available at the deep structure.
- Generalize: We may make general statements about what we believe and how we perceive others and the world. We ignore possible exceptions or special conditions.
- Distort: We may choose to oversimplify or fantasize about what is possible or what has happened.

To recover the information missing as a result of deletions, generalizations and distortions, Grinder and Bandler identified twelve different patterns with corresponding questions and called this the meta model. The meta model is about being more specific – chunking down – to get a better understanding of the person's model of the world. All human communication has the potential to be ambiguous, which can lead to problems. The purpose of the questions is to cut through this ambiguity to access the missing information for both the client and the coach. The goal is to gain a better understanding of the client's deep structure and to make better sense of the communication.

Although based on the work of two therapists, the meta model has much wider applications – wherever two or more people are engaged in communicating – whether at work, at play, within the family or in personal relations.

Once mastered, the meta model is a powerful and useful tool. However, it does take practice to master the questioning process. It must be undertaken with a high degree of rapport – the client must feel safe and not pressured – and used with moderation. Before asking any of my clients, students, colleagues or family members meta model questions, I make sure that they are comfortable in my presence and have a feeling of security. I often ask them the following: "May I ask you a question?" If they respond negatively, I do not pursue it. Instead, I listen to the presuppositions and metaphors in their choice of words to get a clearer understanding of their model of the world.

A first step in learning how to use the meta model is to identify the patterns in your own conversations and practice developing the questions that recover the lost information. As an exercise, you may wish to write a few paragraphs about your career, your family life or your views of life in general. Then identify the meta model patterns and subsequent questions. Make sure you honestly answer these questions and notice if new understandings or possibilities are opened up.

Meta model examples

As you read the following examples and their corresponding questions, you must be sure to place yourself in the role of the person asking the questions. Notice how what is said limits the other person's model of the world, your understanding of his model of the world, as well as your own model of the world if you accept without question what has been said. Also notice how the questions recover lost information or expand possibilities.

Deletions
- **Simple deletion:** Something is left out.

  Example: "I am mad."

  Question to recover lost information: "About what?"

- **Unspecified referential index**: The person(s) or object to which the statement refers is unspecified or not clear.

  Examples: "They rejected my business proposal." "They rejected it."

  Questions to recover lost information: "Who did?" or "Rejected what?"

- **Comparative deletions:** A comparison is made, but what is being compared is unclear. The sentence will often contain words such as: good, bad, better, best, worst, more, less, most, least.

Examples: "This approach is better." "What you are asking me to do is difficult."

Question to recover lost information: "Compared with what or whom?"

- **Unspecified verb:** In this case, it is not clear how something was done.

  Example: "They rejected my business proposal." I have used the same example from the unspecified referential index to illustrate that sometimes several things may have been deleted, distorted or generalized. You must decide which line of questioning will yield the most information.

  Question to recover lost information: "How, specifically?"

- **Nominalizations:** A process has been turned into a "thing." Nominalizations are nouns, yet you cannot physically touch them or put them in the trunk of your car. Examples of nominalizations are: communication, relationship, leadership, management, respect, truth, freedom, depression, fear love, happiness, and so forth. Our task here is to ask a question so that the process can be rediscovered.

  Example: "The communication in our family is poor."

  Question to recover lost information: "How would you like to communicate?" Notice that there is also a comparative deletion here, and we might also ask: "Poor compared with what?"

Generalizations

- **Universal quantifiers:** Universal quantifiers are typically words such as: all, every, never, always, only, everyone, everything, no one, and so on.

  Example: "My boss never gives me credit for what I do."

  Questions to recover lost information: We can exaggerate the generalization or use a counter example. "Never?" or "Has there ever been a time when your boss has given you credit?"

- **Modal operators of possibility or necessity:** Words that refer to possibility or necessity or that reflect internal states of intensity tied to our rules in life. Modal operators of possibility include words such as can/can't, may/may not, possible/impossible. Modal operators of necessity include words and phrases such as should/shouldn't, must/must not, have to, need to, it is necessary.

  Example: "I can't do this now."

  Questions to recover lost information: The key is to challenge the limitation. "What would happen if you did?" or "What prevents you?"

Example: "I must accept what is given to me."

Question to recover lost information: "What would happen if you didn't?"

These questions restore choice and move your client from being at effect to being at cause.

Distortions

- **Mind reading:** In this case, the speaker claims to know what another person believes, feels or thinks.

  Example: "My boss is not pleased with my work."

  Questions to recover lost information: For this pattern, we simply ask: "How do you know?" "How specifically do you know your boss is not pleased with your work?"

- **Lost performative:** Value judgments are made and it is not clear who has made them.

  Example: "This is the right way to get ahead in this company."

  Questions to recover lost information: "According to whom?" "How do you know it is the right way?"

- **Cause–effect:** The speaker establishes a cause–effect relationship between two events or actions. Common constructions include: if/then, because, makes, compels, causes.

  Example: "When you look at me that way, I feel unimportant."

  Question to recover lost information: "How does the way I look at you cause you to choose to feel unimportant?" You could also use a counter example.

- **Complex equivalence:** In this situation, two disparate experiences are interpreted as being synonymous. These two experiences could be joined by words such as: therefore, means, implies.

  Example: "My boss walked into his office without saying good morning; therefore, he is not pleased with my work."

  Questions to recover lost information: "How does not saying good morning mean that your boss is not pleased with your work?" "Have you ever been preoccupied by family or business pressures and forgotten to say good morning to your colleagues?"

- **Presuppositions:** Some part of the sentence presupposes or implies the existence or non-existence of something – a concept, an object, a person – while not explicitly stating it.

Example: "When will you demonstrate leadership for your team?" This question presupposes that you do not demonstrate leadership. If you answer the question directly, you will be digging an even deeper hole for yourself.

Questions to recover lost information: "What leads you to believe that I do not demonstrate leadership?" "How is it that I do not demonstrate leadership?"

Ask "How?" rather than "Why?"

Notice that none of the questions in the meta model begins with "why." When you ask someone a "why" question, often they feel they have to defend what they have said or done, making excuses or rationalizing their behavior. This provides little potential for resolving the issue. Asking "how" gives you an understanding of the process and "how" the problem arose and thus more information and understanding.

4.7. MILTON MODEL

The meta model assists a client in being more specific or precise about her problem; as a result, she begins to discover possible resources or solutions to her problem. When it was first proposed, Gregory Batson, an expert on communication systems theory and anthropology, was enthusiastic about this approach. He was well aware of the work of Milton Erickson, who was also getting great results with his clients, but in a different way – by being artfully vague rather than specific – the exact opposite of the meta model. Batson encouraged John Grinder and Richard Bandler to meet with Erickson and discover why he was so successful. Their description of Erickson's methods became known as the *Milton model* – an approach opposite to the meta model, yet an equally useful tool for personal change and improving human communication.

> The Milton model is a way of using language to induce and maintain trance in order to contact hidden resources of our personality. It follows the way the mind works naturally. Trance is a state where you are highly motivated to learn from your unconscious mind in an inner directed way. It is not a passive state, nor are you under another's influence. There is co-operation between client and therapist, the client's responses letting the therapist know what to do next.
>
> – from *Introducing NLP: Psychological Skills for Understanding and Influencing People*, Joseph O'Connor and John Seymour (Hammersmith, London: Thorsons, 1995, pp. 113–4).

When a person is having problems, it is usually because she has run out of conscious resources. She does not know what to do, what she needs or how to access resources. Trance bypasses the conscious mind and makes the resources of the unconscious mind available. Most significant and long-lasting change takes place at the unconscious level. Each of us has a useful personal history, filled with experiences, knowledge and resources that can be drawn upon, if only we knew how to tap into them.

Milton Erickson

Milton Erickson was generally regarded as the foremost hypnotherapist of his time. He worked with trance and cleverly structured sentences full of vague meanings to help his clients discover how to address their problems and to realize that they already had the necessary coping resources within them. The basis of Erickson's success was his sensory acuity, his ability to read non-verbal behavior, his ability to establish rapport with his clients, his skill with language patterns and his beliefs about his clients. Some of his beliefs appear in the list of NLP presuppositions. For example:

- Every behavior has a positive intention.
- This is the best choice available to a person given the circumstances as they see it.
- Respect for the other person's model of the world.
- Resistance in a client is due to a lack of rapport. Put another way, there are no resistant clients, only inflexible therapists.

Erickson made great use of embedded suggestions, metaphors, anchoring, re-framing and submodalities. He would begin by pacing a client's experience and then lead her into trance, or *downtime*. In NLP terms, *uptime* is when your senses are focused on the outside world, while downtime is related to your inner thoughts. The meta model is associated with uptime (i.e., who, what, how, specifically), while the Milton model is associated with downtime. As we carry out our daily activities, we are continually cycling through uptime and downtime and are often somewhere in between.

Pacing and leading

To *pace* a client, begin by matching and mirroring her physiology, choice of words and tone of voice. Next, make reference to what she would most likely be seeing, hearing, feeling or thinking (for example, "As you notice the lights slowly dimming…" or "As you hear my voice…" or "As you feel the chair on your back…" or "As you wonder…"). Be sure you speak slowly in a soft tone, and pace your speech to her breathing. To *lead* her into downtime, begin to focus her attention inward by saying something such as: "You may notice how easy it is to close your eyes whenever you wish to feel more relaxed…"

Milton model: hypnotic language patterns

The topic of trance and hypnosis is vast. This section focuses on the Milton model. For more information on hypnosis, the Milton model and other hypnotic techniques, an excellent resource is *Hypnosis: A Comprehensive Guide* by Tad James (The Cromwell Press, 2000).

The Milton model hypnotic language patterns encourage the listener to move away from detail and content and move to higher levels of thinking and deeper states of mind. Some patterns are used to distract the conscious mind and establish a trance state, a state of downtime or relaxation in the body. Other patterns are used to loosen the listener's model of the world – from which he is expressing his current behaviors – and to consider a more expansive interpretation of what is possible.

You will notice that many of these language patterns are identical to those of the meta model. The difference is that for the meta model, the client is being vague, and, as a coach, you ask specific questions to assist her in getting clarity on her issue or problem. With the Milton model, you use some of the same language patterns, but this time you wish to be vague so the client can easily go into trance or from the vague suggestions and linguistic presuppositions she may choose a course of action that will address her problem.

The following are the Milton model hypnotic language patterns:

- **Mind read:** Claiming to know another's thoughts or feelings without specifying the how you came to that knowledge.

  "I know that you believe…" or "I know you're thinking…."

- **Lost performative:** Expressing value judgments without identifying the one doing the judging.

  "Breathing is good."

- **Cause–effect:** Implies one thing leads to or causes another; that there is sequence of cause and effect and a flow in time. Includes such parallel phrases as: "If/then; as you/then you; because/then."

  "If you can hear my voice, then you can learn many things."

- **Complex equivalence:** This phrase attributes meaning to something that may or may not have a "cause" capability.

  "Being here means you will change easily."

- **Presupposition:** The linguistic equivalent of assumptions.

  "Will you be changing your attitude, now or later today?" It is assumed the person will change their attitude; the only unknown is when.

- **Universal quantifier:** Universal generalizations without referential index. Includes words such as: everyone, no one, all, every.

  "Everyone is this room is capable of changing their attitude." "All your dreams are possible."

- **Modal operator:** Words that refer to possibility or necessity or that reflect internal states of intensity tied to our rules in life.

  "You can make choices." "You must resolve this issue."

- **Nominalization:** Words that are formed as nouns and that are shorthand for processes.

  "People can come to new understandings." Here *understandings* is used as a noun and is shorthand to describe the continuing experience of understanding or making sense of something.

- **Unspecified verb:** Implies action without describing how the action has taken place or will take place.

  "You have resolved the problem."

- **Tag question:** A question following another more direct, emphatic statement or question, designed to soften resistance. It is used to ensure that the listener has or will actually manifest the implied action. It has the structure of a question and often the tonality of a statement.

  "Your perception of life is changing, *isn't it.*"

- **Lack of referential index:** An expression without specific reference to any portion of the speaker's or listener's experience.

  "People can change."

- **Comparative deletion** (unspecified comparison): A comparison is made without specific reference to what or to whom it is being compared.

  "You will enjoy it more." "That one is better."

- **Pace current experience:** Using sensory-grounded, behaviorally specific information to describe current experience.

  "You are reading this book." "Your eyes are open."

- **Double bind:** Invites choice within a larger context of "no choice."

"Do you want to begin now or later?" "Do you want to go into trance before or after you sit down?"

- **Embedded commands:** This is a command that forms part of a larger sentence that is marked by using italics or a subtle change in voice tonality or body language and is picked up by the reader's or listener's unconscious.

"I will not suggest to you that *change is easy*." "Do you think you should *tell your friends about this book*?" "You can *learn* this material *easily*."

- **Conversational postulate:** These are questions that operate at multiple levels. Although they require only a simple yes or no answer, they invite you to engage in an activity in some way. Often they contain an embedded command.

"Can you *open the door*?" "Can you choose to *change*?"

- **Extended quote:** Is a rambling context for the delivery of information that may be in the format of a command.

"Many years ago, I remember meeting a wise old man who taught me many useful things. I cherished all of his advice. I remember one particular day when he said that as a youngster he had been told: 'Change is easy and can be fun.'"

- **Selectional restriction violation:** Attributing intelligence or animation to inanimate objects.

"Your chair can support you as you make these changes." "Your diary tells interesting stories."

- **Lack of specificity:**

  o Phonological: *your* and *you're*. In this example, there are two words with the same sound, but with a different meaning. "Your (or you're) changing state."

  o Syntactic: more than one possible meaning. The syntax is uncertain within the context, i.e., are the words used as adjectives, verbs or nouns? Examples: *shooting stars, leadership shows*.

  o Scope: The context does not reveal the scope to which a verb or modifier applies. "Speaking to you as a changed person..." Who is the changed person? – the person speaking or the person listening? "The old men and women..." Here it is unclear whether we are talking about old men and old women or old men and women in general.

  o Punctuation: is unexpected and does not "follow the rules." For example, improper pauses, rambling sentences, incomplete sentences, all of which ultimately force the listener to "mind read." "Hand me your watch how quickly you will resolve this issue."

- **Utilization:** This pattern takes advantage of everything in the listener's experience (both internal and external environments) to support the intention of the speaker.

Client says: "I don't understand."

Response: "That's right, – you don't understand, – yet, because you've not taken that one deep breath that will allow the information to fall easily and comfortably into place."

Or perhaps while working with a client, one of your colleagues mistakenly opens the door and inadvertently interrupts you. Instead of getting frustrated and annoyed with your colleague, you could say to your client, "Why not allow the door's opening to be an opportunity to invite new ideas and thoughts into your life?"

These patterns are not limited to trance or personal change work. You will come across all of them in everyday speech. For example, how often do you see advertising that refers to a product as "better"? Political speeches are vague and lack specificity in their promises. In corporate settings, we discuss nominalizations such as leadership, communication, respect and education as if they are tangible objects, and we most often ignore the underlying process that should really be addressed.

4.8. METAPHORS

A metaphor is an indirect way of communicating through a story or figure of speech. It may reveal the culture of an organization or the deeper thoughts of an individual. It can also imply a comparison (be quiet as a mouse) or parallel the patterns of a problem to offer solutions or suggestions (a fairy tale: *The Boy Who Cried Wolf*). In NLP, metaphors include similes, parables, clichés and allegories, and are rich in their ability to enhance communication. Metaphors are part of everyone's life, from the bedtime story, through the parables in the Bible, to the way you think of yourself and the way you dress.

Deep structure of thought

The deep structure of thought is based on feelings, memories, beliefs and values, and is revealed through our behaviors and our choice of words. In individuals, this deep structure is referred to as our personality; in organizations, it is called "corporate culture."

At work, you may hear an individual say, "we need some ammunition," "put on your flak jacket," "rally the troops," "bring out the big artillery" or "we need to outflank them." These are figures of speech analogous to wartime, and reveal the deep beliefs of an individual – or a group – that work is viewed as war. Other people may view their work environment as a "zoo" or as something to be endured, and their actions and words will reflect this. The metaphors you have for life, work or home will, in turn, color how you see things. They will surface in your behaviors and in the words you use, and will influence your interactions with others.

Understanding a person's or an organization's metaphor can provide insights to their inner feelings, memories, beliefs and values, and can provide you with an opportunity to be of assistance. At one practitioner training session, I was not sure of a particular woman's metaphor until she said the following in one of our open discussions: "I just got a new car. It's so perfect," she said, "that I feel like leaving it in the parking lot and not using it so it will remain perfect." I asked if I might ask her a question. She agreed and I asked, "So how much longer are you going to put your life in a parking lot, waiting for perfection?" She paused, and had nothing immediate to say in response. However, her physical reaction made it obvious that this question had given her great insight into how she was currently living her life.

Consider the following example of two NLP trainers. One sees himself as a guide – a person who helps people along life's journey – and the other views herself as a repository of NLP knowledge and techniques. I am almost certain you would see distinct differences in their behaviors, during and outside of class. If we are not provided with this initial knowledge of how each trainer views him- or herself, would it not still be possible to observe significant differences in their behaviors and to guess the metaphor that each carries?

People's behaviors give us insights into the metaphors they are living – if we are paying attention. Your metaphor may function at the spiritual level (purpose in life), as your identity (who you are) or as a belief or value that you hold to be important. No matter which it is, it will have a distinct influence on your strategies and hence the behaviors you manifest.

Working with metaphors

If a person or organization finds that their metaphors are not serving them, those metaphors can be changed to trigger different ways of thinking or to see the issue from a different perspective. As a coach or trainer, you may assist a team of business people in changing its war metaphor – indicating conflict – to a sports metaphor – indicating competition. You can suggest new metaphors such as, "move the ball forward," "avoid being offside," "need a big play." Or you may wish to take a non-competitive, win-win perspective and choose metaphors that help each person see how he can support the others. Changing metaphors often gives you new insights and opportunities to pursue and is a useful way to transfer learning or concepts between different contexts.

Metaphors can be used in situations where you would like your listener to detach from his current situation and consider other possibilities. This is especially so in giving presentations, teaching, negotiating, managing, coaching – wherever there is potential for resistance, opposition or conflict. Metaphors provide the speaker with helpful and useful communication and negotiation tools. It is difficult to argue with a good metaphor.

To determine a client's metaphor, listen to the words he uses and observe his behaviors. Alternatively, have him draw a picture of how he sees himself in the world, at work or at home. You can also ask him to draw a picture of how he would like to be in the future. This can be a very instructive exercise for the coach as well as the client, as you now work on bridging the two metaphors.

Communicating with the unconscious mind

Metaphors communicate indirectly. An interesting story bypasses any conscious blocks or resistance and slips into the unconscious mind, where it triggers an unconscious search for meaning, resources and learnings. This is why fairy tales can have such a great impact on children. Metaphors are an effective way of communicating with someone in a trance.

Metaphors can be developed for a general audience (i.e., a presentation), or for a specific person. While listening to a metaphor, your unconscious mind will seek meaning and learnings appropriate for you.

Creating a metaphor

A successful metaphor must first pace the client's current experience by using the same sequence of steps, representational systems and submodalities as his present state. If, for example, the first step in your client's strategy is a big, bright picture, the first step in your metaphor should be a visually big, bright picture. The content does not have to be the same – in fact, the greater the differences and the more interesting you can make the subject matter, the better. What is needed is a smooth transition to the desired state – a state that will have its own sequence of steps, representational systems and submodalities.

To make the metaphor interesting, select something of interest to your client. One client with whom I worked did not take care of himself. He had a poor diet, did not see a doctor for annual checkups and, as a result, was in poor physical condition. In our conversations, I discovered that his hobby was build-ing and racing cars. The parallel I drew for him was how important it was for his racing car to be in top shape through regular servicing in order to maintain its peak performance.

The following is a general method for creating a metaphor for your client:

1. Determine and verify with your client his present state.

2. Assist your client in deciding upon an appropriate outcome or desired state.

3. Choose a subject area for the metaphor. The more different from the issue being addressed the better. Choose a subject that is definitely of interest to your client and of which you have some knowledge and competency.

4. Pace your client's current experience by using the same sequence of steps, representational systems and submodalities as his present state. That is, for each aspect of the real life situation, select a matching element in the metaphor.

5. Decide on the transition to the desired state. If there is a surprising twist, you have an even better metaphor with which to work.

6. If installing a new strategy, ensure the desired state has the appropriate sequence of steps, representational systems and submodalities.

7. Use Milton model language and appropriate voice tonality. The more ab-stract the language, the more freedom you give your client's unconscious mind to determine the most appropriate course of action. Use embedded commands to assist your client's unconscious mind.

5.

Making Personal Improvements

5.1. SUBMODALITIES

Modalities and submodalities

We have five basic senses: visual, auditory, kinesthetic, olfactory and gustatory. As we have learned, these are referred to as representational systems or modalities. For each of these modalities, we make finer distinctions. We might describe a picture as being black and white or color, and the colors bright or dim. Sounds may be loud or soft, or coming from a particular direction. Feelings may be in different parts of the body or have different temperatures. Smells may be pleasant or offensive, strong or light. Taste may be sweet or bitter, strong or mild. These finer distinctions are called submodalities and define how we interpret our internal representations. People have known about and worked with submodalities for centuries. Aristotle referred to qualities of the senses, but did not use the term submodalities. Generally, we work with only three submodalities – visual, auditory and kinesthetic. However, you may be working with a client on an issue where the olfactory or gustatory submodalities play a major role – perhaps the client is on a diet and food is an issue.

Example submodalities for visual, auditory and kinesthetic are presented in the table on the next page.

Illustrative exercises

The following two exercises illustrate how submodalities work. You will be asked to make a picture in your mind (an internal representation). For some of us, the pictures we make in our minds are very clear. For others, the picture is not clear; there is only a general sense of it being there, and if we were asked questions about its qualities (submodalities) we would be able to answer

EXAMPLE SUBMODALITIES		
Visual	**Auditory**	**Kinesthetic**
Black & white or color	Loud or soft	Strong or weak
Near or far	Near or far	Large area or small area
Bright or dim	Internal or external	Weight: heavy or light
Location[1]	Location	Location
Size of picture	Stereo or mono	Texture: smooth or rough
Associated/dissociated[2]	Fast or slow	Constant or intermittent
Focused or defocused	High or low pitch	Temperature: hot or cold
Framed or unbounded	Verbal or tonal	Size
Movie or still	Rhythm	Shape
If a movie – is it fast/ normal/slow?	Clarity	Pressure
Three-dimensional or flat	Pauses	Vibration

1. Your client may think of location as a particular place, e.g. his house or backyard. For sub-modalities, this is not what is meant by location. The location submodality refers to where the internal representation is located. For the visual submodality, the mental picture could be directly in front, to the left, up and to the right, and so on. For sound, it could be located in front of you, behind you or it might surround you. For a feeling, it could be in a particular part of the body or throughout your body.

2. The visual submodality Associated/Dissociated is very important and refers to whether you can see yourself in the picture (visual internal representation). You are associated if you cannot see yourself in the picture. That is, you are "looking through your own eyes," fully participating in the event. If you can see yourself in the picture, then you are said to be dissociated.

If you are associated in a memory, then your feelings (happy, sad, fearful) about that memory will be more intense. If you are dissociated, this is more like watching a movie of your life rather than being involved, and any feelings will be less intense or non-existent. If your client is addressing an issue that is very emotional or traumatic, it may be advantageous to have him view this memory from a dissociated perspective.

accurately. To keep the exercises simple, we will only work with the visual submodalities.

Exercise 1:

Get comfortable, close your eyes and form a picture in your mind of someone whose company you really enjoy. When you get this picture, notice the submodalities. That is, is the picture bright or dim, where is it located, are you associated or dissociated, and so on. Once you have done this, break state – open your eyes and clear your mind by stretching and looking around.

Again, close your eyes and this time, form a picture in your mind of someone whose presence you do not enjoy. Notice the submodalities of this picture. Once you have done this, break state.

Were you able to identify several submodalities that were different in the two internal representations?

Generally, the internal representations of people whose company we enjoy will have similar submodalities as will the internal representations of people whose company we do not enjoy. The two sets of internal representations, however, will be different – in some way – from each other. This sameness and differences in submodalities allow us to code our experiences and give meaning to our past and future memories.

Submodalities are useful and fun to play with. For example, if the internal representation of someone you do not enjoy being with is large, and up close (i.e., "in your face"), what do you think would happen if you made the picture in your mind smaller and pushed it away to a more comfortable distance? You may still not necessarily like this person; however, you may find them not quite as overbearing.

Exercise 2:

For this exercise, close your eyes and think of a time when you were very happy. Once you have a picture of this, make it very dark, shrink it down to a small picture and push it far away. When you do this, what do you notice about your feelings of happiness? Are they reduced or did they disappear? You have just learned an effective method of removing happiness from your life – take all your happy memories and make the pictures very dark, small and far away. Of course, I am not seriously suggesting you do this. However, there are some people who tend to discount their happy memories by doing just that – making them dark, small and far away, while making their unpleasant memories big and bright and close. And how do you think they live their lives?

These two examples illustrate that the submodalities you use to store your memories give meaning to those memories. You cannot change an event that has already happened; however, by adjusting the submodalities of the memory, you can change how you perceive it and respond to it. This is also true for envisioning and imagining future events.

Key building blocks of NLP techniques

Submodalities are key components of many of the NLP techniques. Submodalities, by themselves or as part of other techniques, have been used to assist people to stop smoking, eat more of certain foods and less of others, address compulsion issues, change beliefs and values, enhance motivation, move from stress to relaxation, address phobias and many other personal issues.

A technique using submodalities

You can use this technique to assist yourself or your client for any of the following situations:

- You eat a food that is not healthy for you (call this behavior A). You would like to remove this food from your diet. Identify a similar food that you do not eat at all (behavior B).
- You eat too much of a particular food (behavior A). You would like to eat less of this food. Let us suppose you eat this food every day and would like to reduce it to once a week. Behavior B would be a similar food that you eat once a week.
- You do not eat a food that you would like to add to your diet (behavior A). Identify a similar food that you eat on a regular basis (behavior B).
- You feel insecure when you give business presentations (behavior A). You would like to present with confidence and feel good about yourself. Identify a similar situation, where you are the type of presenter that you would like to be – perhaps you coach a children's sports team and speak in front of them with confidence (behavior B).
- There is a co-worker with whom you do not communicate well (behavior A). You would like to have a more meaningful and warmer communication with this person (you cannot change other people, you can only change how you perceive other people and then how you choose to behave in their presence). Identify someone with whom you do get along well (behavior B).

Notice in the above that I have labeled each of the undesired behaviors as A and the desired behaviors as B. Now proceed with the following steps:

1. Have your client close his eyes and think of a situation in which he exhibited

the undesired behavior (behavior A). Elicit the submodalities (visual, auditory and kinesthetic) for this memory (internal representation).[3]

This exercise should be done quickly and spontaneously. There is no need to have an extensive conversation with your client. You can say: "Do you have a picture? Is it black and white or color?" "Is it near or far?" Continue for the other visual submodalities. Then ask if there are any sounds. If not, ask if there are any feelings. If not, you are finished. In pertinent cases, determine the auditory and kinesthetic submodalities. Make brief notes to remember your client's submodalities.

Generally we elicit the visual submodalities first, followed by auditory and then kinesthetic, even if the client's preferred representational system is something other than visual.

2. Have your client break state.

3. Have your client close his eyes and think of a situation in which he exhibited the desired behavior (behavior B). Elicit the submodalities for this memory.

4. Have your client break state.

5. Compare the submodalities from steps one and three (column two with column three, if you have made a table) to determine which submodalities are different – these are called the *critical submodalities*.

   This process is called *contrastive analysis*. In column one, place an asterisk next to those submodalities that are different, as these are the only submodalities you will need to change in step six.

6. Have your client close his eyes and recall the internal representation for behavior A (the undesired behavior). Instruct him to keep the content of the internal representation constant as he changes the critical submodalities to those of behavior B. This is called *mapping across*.

   To illustrate, assume the content of my visual internal representation for behavior A is a picture of spinach and that the submodalities are small and dark. Assume behavior B is a picture of lettuce and that the submodalities are large and bright. To map across, I would continue to see spinach and at the same time change the small, dark picture to a large, bright picture.

---

3. You may wish to set up a table with three columns. In the first column, list the names for the visual, auditory and kinesthetic submodalities; in column two, write the submodalities as described by your client for behavior A (from step one); in column three, write the submodalities for behavior B (from step three).

One at a time, tell your client which submodalities to change, and as he does, watch him carefully to note which submodality causes the greatest change in his physiology. Once he has changed each of the critical submodalities, you can compare notes with him to determine which submodality had the greatest impact. This submodality is called the *driver*. Once the driver submodality is changed, it is not unusual for the client to say, "The rest of the submodalities have changed!"

Often the driver is a visual submodality and one of the following: location, distance, associated/dissociated, brightness, color/black and white, or focus. For different contexts, your client may have different drivers.

7.   Break state and test by future pacing.

Swish pattern

The *swish pattern* is a useful technique to help people address an unwanted behavior response to a specific stimulus. This is based on changing key submodalities. Compulsive or obsessive behaviors such as an uncontrollable desire to bite your nails, smoke, eat certain foods, or habits, or an unresourceful response – perhaps your reaction when asked to give a presentation – are often linked with a specific stimulus, trigger or cue image.

As an example, I used this technique with a woman who was a model. For many of her modeling assignments, she had a five-hour drive to Toronto. Along the way, she would snack on potato chips. First, I verified with her that this was an unwanted behavior, also checking that there was no secondary gain. When asked what she would like to do as an alternate behavior, she replied, "Eat apples." My task was to unlink the initial mental cue image (seeing herself driving to Toronto) from the act of eating potato chips and, instead, link it to eating an apple.

1.   Have your client identify a) a specific behavior that she wishes to change, and b) the cue image that starts the process.

2.   Have your client identify a new self-image with the desired behavior that satisfies the positive intent of the undesired behavior. Have her generate a picture of this new self-image.

Your task now is to link the cue image in step one with the new self-image in step two.

3.   Check the ecology of the new self-image and associated behavior(s).

Have your client assess the impact of this new behavior on herself, her family, friends, colleagues and community. What will she have to give up or take on?

4. Identify at least two submodalities that when changed reduce the desire for the behavior in step one and increase the desire for the new self-image in step two.

    Ask your client to form a picture of the behavior in step one, and then have her adjust different submodalities and notice which ones reduce the desire for this behavior. For example, she may find that reducing the brightness and defocusing the picture reduces the desire for this behavior. The submodalities should be those that vary over a continuous range, i.e., brightness, size or focus.

    Now ask your client to get a picture of the new self-image and behavior (from step two), and notice if the desire for this behavior is increased as the submodalities identified in the previous paragraph are changed in the opposite direction. For instance, does increasing the brightness and improving the focus make the new self-image in step two more compelling?

    It is possible to perform the swish pattern with an auditory or kinesthetic cue. In these cases, you would use auditory or kinesthetic submodalities. However, the process is easiest if you use a visual cue.

    Remember to break state when switching between behaviors.

    For the rest of the procedure, I will assume that the critical submodalities are brightness and focus.

5. Have your client take the cue picture and make it big, bright and clearly focused. In a corner of this picture (let's say the lower right-hand corner), have your client put a small, dark and defocused picture of the new self-image and related behavior.

    Your client should be associated in the cue picture (i.e., cannot see herself in the picture, she is looking through her own eyes). The picture of the new self-image must be dissociated to create an end state that is motivating and appealing. An associated picture gives your client the feeling that she has already made the change, and therefore it will not be motivating for her.

6. Have your client make the cue picture smaller, darker and defocused as the picture of the new self-image gets bigger, brighter and focused. Continue until the cue picture is a small dark, defocused picture in the lower right-hand corner of a big bright, focused picture of the new self-image.

7. Have your client take a moment to enjoy this new self-image and the resources that she now has available to her.

8. Break state. Have your client repeat steps five, six and seven, but this time have her do step six faster.

It is important to break state after step seven. You want to create a compelling direction from the cue picture to the new self-image. If you did not break state, then you would set up a cycle where the new self-image leads back to the cue picture.

9. Have your client repeat steps five, six and seven until she has done it at least seven times and step six takes a fraction of a second to complete.

    This is why it is called swish pattern – in less time than it takes to quickly say "swish," your client has completed step six. Speed is essential in this step.

10. Test and future pace. Have your client think of the cue. Does she now think of the new self-image and related behaviors?

5.2. ANCHORS

The Nobel-award-winning scientist and physiologist Ivan Petrovich Pavlov developed the notion of stimulus response by giving food to his dogs and simultaneously ringing a bell. In time, the dogs came to associate the sound of the bell with food and would salivate when they heard the bell, even if no food was present. Here, the stimulus is the bell and the response is salivating.

In NLP, anchoring refers to a stimulus response, similar to the link that Pavlov established. The stimulus – the anchor or trigger – may come from your external environment. Perhaps this is someone touching your shoulder or seeing a red light, or it may be an internal representation. In either case, it triggers a conscious or unconscious internal response or feeling that may result in a behavioral response.

We all have numerous different anchors. As teenagers, a friend and I spent a week together in Bermuda. While on the trip, I regularly used a popular brand of suntan lotion. Many years later, when I smell the scent of this same suntan lotion, no matter where I am or what I am doing, my fond recollections of that vacation come immediately to mind. This is an example of an external olfactory anchor that generates an instant internal response.

The following are other examples of anchors. Can you add to this list?

- Red traffic light – external visual.
- Police siren – external auditory.
- A gentle touch by a loved one – external kinesthetic.
- The taste of a favorite food – external gustatory.
- During a training course, the facilitator uses the word "test" – external auditory digital (a word).
- An internal visual representation (a picture) of your children – internal visual.

- Your mother says your full name or your childhood nickname in a certain tone of voice – external auditory and auditory digital.

The swish pattern began with a cue picture, or trigger, and linked this to a new self-image with certain behaviors. This is an example of changing a response to an existing anchor or trigger.

Anchors can be very useful, yet they can also be counterproductive. Most anchors operate outside of your conscious awareness and have an impact on your mental state or behavior, despite the fact that you may be unaware of them. Useful anchors are those that generate pleasant memories or put you into a motivated, confident or empowered state, or those that result in a useful behavior: a red light is ahead; you slow and stop the car. Examples of counter-productive anchors are:

- You are a fully functioning adult until you step across the threshold of your parent's house, when you may take on certain less than resourceful behaviors.
- You panic when you are told that your boss wants to see you in her office in five minutes.
- Someone making a comment causes you to remember an unpleasant memory that, in turn, leads to an emotional response.
- Your spouse makes a comment, using a certain tone of voice and body language, and you react in a less than resourceful manner.
- Someone touches you unexpectedly, and this brings up past memories of an unpleasant event.
- At a meeting, a colleague who continually brings up problems without solutions begins to speak, and you think, "Oh no, not again." You begin to tune him out.

Certain venues serve as anchors. These can be intimidating because they arouse certain emotions and are thus threatening to relaxed and open dialogue. As a manager, if you want to have an informal conversation with your staff where they can speak freely, choose a place other than your office – offsite is the best.

Phobias are anchors that trigger a very powerful negative state.

Your client may have an anchor that triggers an unresourceful state. You may be inclined to ask, "Why do you react that way?" but this can result in your client giving reasons and justifying his response. Instead, ask him, "How do you do that?" Now you are looking at it as a process or strategy. If you can identify the trigger and remove it or disrupt the process – called a *pattern interrupt* – you'll find that the rest of the original process will not occur and the strategy will not find completion in the same way it did in the past.

Basic anchoring concepts

You can create anchors to serve you or change those that do not generate the results you want. To do this, you need to understand some basic concepts about anchors.

Anchors can be created naturally or artificially in two ways:

1. In a single occurrence, if it happens during a highly emotional, positive or negative event. For example, your significant other may have taken you to a special place and proposed to you in a very romantic and emotional way. When you return to this location, what comes to mind?

2. Through repetition and the continual association between a stimulus and a response. Repetition is needed if the emotion is weak or there is no emotional involvement at all. Television commercials often link an alcoholic beverage with a pleasant experience. After seeing this advertisement a number of times, you begin to make the pleasant association.

The anchor needs to be:

- Unique, distinct and easy to repeat. It should not have other, previous associations. If touching your thumb and index finger is not something you do routinely, this would be an effective kinesthetic anchor. Saying a word internally – "thinking" the word – in a particular tone of voice would be a good auditory digital and auditory anchor. Selecting a trigger that you inadvertently fire quite often has the potential of dissipating the anchor – rendering it useless in the desired context. Unique anchors or triggers are best and more enduring.

- Linked to a state that is cleanly and completely re-experienced. Your client may wish to create an anchor enabling him to feel confident in certain situations. However, if he is confused about your instructions for setting the anchor, the resulting anchor may generate a response that is a mixture of confidence and confusion.

- Timed just as the state is reaching its peak. As your client recalls a time that he possessed a certain attribute – confidence, for example – the feeling of confidence will begin to get stronger until it reaches a peak. Generally, the anchor should be applied when the response reaches about two-thirds of its peak and held until it peaks. Depending on how fast your client accesses his feelings, the anchor could be applied anywhere from several seconds to ten seconds. Applying the anchor past the peak may result in picking up a weakened or other unwanted state.

The basic steps for anchoring are:

1. Have your client recall a past vivid experience for the state you are anchoring.

2. Apply a specific trigger as the state is reaching its peak.

3. Break state.

4. Test the anchor. When you fire the trigger, does your client go into the state?

5. Repeating steps one through three several times will make the anchor stronger. This is called *stacking* an anchor.

The best state to anchor is a naturally occurring state (for example, you are laughing at a joke you've just heard). The next best state is a past, vivid, highly associated state. To create an anchor for a specific state you have never experienced, think of someone who possesses that quality – this person can be real or imaginary. Imagine stepping into that person's shoes and taking on her physiology and feelings when she is in that state.

To elicit a past memory for anchoring purposes, you can use the following script for yourself or with your client:

> Remember a specific time when you were really _____ (e.g., confident). Close your eyes and fully associate into that memory by going back to that time, putting yourself in your own body, looking through your own eyes, seeing what you saw, hearing what you heard and having the feelings of being really _____.

If you are working with a client, you can also assist her by using a voice tonality that reflects the state she is accessing. If this is an energetic state, your voice tonality should reflect energy.

To maintain an anchor, it should only be fired when necessary, and it should have regular reinforcement. To reinforce or build up an anchor, you can do two things: 1) regularly repeat the process you used to establish the anchor, or 2) if you notice you are naturally experiencing the desired state, fire the trigger to enhance the anchor.

To enhance the strength of the anchor or to associate different resources to the same anchor, you can stack the anchors; that is, repeat the anchoring process several times by eliciting several occurrences of the same or different states, and anchor them with the same trigger.

Anchors can be used to increase productivity and communication potential in a variety of ways. The following are some examples:

Enhance learning and memory

A friend recently took an intensive course designed to prepare participants to write and pass a prestigious certification test. During the classroom period, the instructor distributed peppermints with a very strong taste and smell. He encouraged the participants to place a peppermint in their mouth while they were deep in thought and concentrating on learning the material. After the course, the instructor provided the participants with more peppermints and suggested that they savor one while taking the certification test. The purpose was to take advantage of the association between the environmental cues of taste and smell and the state they were in when learning the material.

Influence the response you trigger in other people

The manner in which you address other people, along with your tone of voice, the words you choose and your body language, has the potential to establish an anchor in other people, especially if this behavior is repeated several times. As an example, suppose you are the speaker at a product presentation. As you speak, you take the same spot on the stage (this is known as a *spatial* anchor), have a specific body language and tone of voice every time the audience agrees with your point of view. During your presentation, you repeat this behavior several times. Finally, to wrap up your presentation, you return to the same spot, assume the same body language and tone of voice and say, "This is the product that will meet your needs." At an unconscious level, the audience will create a positive association with your product and, if it meets their needs, be more inclined to buy it.

This is a useful example. I often see presenters unconsciously setting negative anchors and subsequently associating their product with these anchors.

Presenting your product in a positive light through anchoring is in many ways similar to having your audience respond well to your product because you are dressed appropriately, took time to ensure your slides looked professional, rehearsed your presentation and had your product packaged or laid out in an attractive manner.

Access internal resources whenever you need them

Would it not be useful to call up a specific resource – such as confidence – whenever you felt your confidence waning? Or perhaps you would like to have a variety of resources at your command (confidence, energy, excitement, humor) as you give a presentation. This calls for a *resource* anchor. The steps are as follows.

1. Identify the situation in which you would like to be more resourceful.

2. Identify the resource(s) that you would like to have available. Ensure they are ecological.

3. Establish what the anchor – the trigger or stimulus – will be.

   The anchor should be easy to fire, inconspicuous and only fired when you choose. I prefer to use a kinesthetic anchor. Possible suggestions are: touching your right ear with your right hand, touching your index finger and thumb together or making a fist in a different fashion than you ordinarily do.

4. Think of a time when you experienced that resource and elicit the state. You can use the elicitation script mentioned above.

5. When you feel the state achieving about two-thirds of its peak, fire the anchor and hold it until it peaks, then release.

6. Break state.

7. Repeat steps four and five at least five times to establish and stack the anchor.

8. Test the association by firing the anchor and confirming that you are experiencing the desired state. If not, or if the state is not strong enough, repeat steps four and five.

The following are some variations on the above:

- You may wish to have several different resources associated with a specific anchor. For example, in addition to confidence, you may also wish to be energetic and excited. In this case, at step seven, introduce a different resource with the same trigger.

- To make the elicited state stronger in step four, you may wish to adjust the submodalities or take on a physiology that reflects the desired state.

Remember, you cannot change other people. However, by being more resourceful, you can choose to adopt different behaviors when dealing with them. For others to continue participating in your communication, they will have to modify their behaviors or withdraw from the communication.

Replace a problem state with a powerful positive state (collapse anchors)

Sometimes, when an anchor fires, you may find yourself in a problem state when you really would have liked to react in a more positive way. Perhaps when your spouse makes a comment in a certain tone of voice, you react by becoming angry, sulking or withdrawing. Your boss may look at you in a certain way, resulting in you feeling dismissed or stupid. Or perhaps when you are in the presence of your parents, you feel as if you are a child again. *Collapsing* anchors is a technique that can resolve problems such as these.

The process of collapsing anchors is based on the notion that if one anchor is much stronger than another, and both are fired at the same time, the stronger anchor will overwhelm the weaker one. This technique uses a kinesthetic anchor; therefore, you should have your client's permission to touch her knuckles (or some other appropriate spot) before proceeding. If you don't do this, you may surprise her and she may not feel safe – instead, she'll be wondering how or where you may touch her next. This process can also be done with a visual or auditory anchor, but I find that a kinesthetic anchor works best.

1. Identify the problem state or experience.

2. Have your client close her eyes and recall the problem state or experience, fully associated, looking through her own eyes, seeing what she saw, hearing what she heard and feeling what she felt at the time. Anchor by touching a specific knuckle.

3. Break state.

4. Test the negative "problem" anchor to ensure it is established by firing the anchor. Your client should be feeling and taking on the physiology of the problem state.

5. Break state.

6. Have your client identify a positive resource state or several different resource states.

   Ask your client how she would like to react or feel instead. I find a number of practitioners tell their clients how they ought to feel, but this originates from the practitioner's model of the world and may not be useful for the client.

7. Have your client recall the positive, resourceful state, fully associated, looking through her own eyes, seeing what she saw, hearing what she heard and feeling what she felt at the time. Anchor by touching a different knuckle.

8. Break state.

9. Repeat steps six to eight until you have built up a powerful positive anchor.

   You can stack the same positive state or stack a number of different states. The key is to ensure that this positive anchor is bigger and more powerful than the negative anchor. Use the same knuckle, even if you are using different positive resource states.

10. Have your client close her eyes while you fire both anchors at the same time.

    Carefully observe your client's physiology. You are looking for some shift – signs of change or confusion – to indicate that the integration is complete. This shift may be obvious: her head may jerk back, or her face may become flushed; or less obvious: her eyelids may flutter slightly or her hands twitch. Each client will react differently.

11. Once you have observed this shift, release the negative anchor by removing your finger from that knuckle.

12. Hold the positive anchor for an additional five seconds, then release.

13. Test and future pace.

    Have your client imagine a future situation, where in the past she would have reacted with the unresourceful state. What happens now as she thinks of this future event?

Link states by creating a path (chain anchors)

Occasionally, the problem state may be very strong compared with the desired state, or the perceived distance between the two states is large. For some people, moving from procrastination to becoming motivated is a great leap. In this case, it is advisable to develop some stepping stones between the disparate states (as we would to cross a stream). *Chaining* anchors establishes a neurological pathway that assists you or your client to easily and unconsciously move through a sequence of different states to a desired end state.

1. Identify the undesired present state.

2. Decide on the positive end state.

3. Design the chain by deciding what intermediate states will best lead to the end state.

    The fewer intermediate states the better. Often there are two or three: the state immediately after the problem state where, in the past, your client may have begun to explore doing something different; the state just before the positive, resourceful end state where your client realizes she can indeed reach her desired outcome; and possibly a state between these two that builds resources or momentum toward the desired state.

4. Elicit and anchor each state separately, beginning with the present state through the end state. Make sure that you break state so that your client comes out of her previous state prior to anchoring the next one.

I use the knuckles because there are, conveniently, four knuckles. If you find you need more than four steps, use the knuckles on both hands.

5. Test each state.

6. Chain each state together by firing #1 and, at its peak, firing #2. When #2 reaches its peak, fire #3, and so on.

   All the anchors must be connected. If you lift your finger off knuckle #1 before you fire #2, there will be no connection. If you leave your finger on knuckles #1 and #2 simultaneously for too long of a time, you will potentially collapse these anchors. There must be an overlap, and it must be brief.

7. Test. Fire anchor #1 and your client should end up in the final, positive end state.

8. Future pace.

5.3. REFRAMING

A picture frame places borders or boundaries around what you can see in a picture. In a similar fashion, the frames of reference you choose as a result of your beliefs about yourself and others, your perceived role in life, and your perceived limitations in skills or abilities can limit what you see as possible; alternatively, they can open up all sorts of possibilities. You (and others, if you allow them) are continually setting time frames, psychological boundaries and physical limits on what you imagine you can or can't do – often without any real thought about the consequences or the reality of those limitations.

Changing the frame of an experience can have a major influence on how you perceive, interpret and react to that experience. Knowing you have one hour to complete a task will most likely result in a different emotional state, approach and quality of work than if you know you have one week to accomplish the same task. This illustrates how a change in frame – in this case a time frame – can have a significant impact on the choices you make. In NLP, changing the frame of reference is called *reframing*. The purpose of reframing is to help people experience their own thoughts, beliefs and actions – and the impact of these – from a different perspective, with the potential to become more resourceful in finding solutions to their problems. Reframing by itself seldom resolves the problem. Instead, it offers the potential of "softening up" the problem so that its resolution is more feasible.

Reframing goes on all around us:
- Politicians are masters at reframing. It seems no matter what happens, they can create a positive spin for themselves or a negative spin for their opponents.

- You may be frustrated at your wife for inviting the elderly gentleman next door for supper. However, when she points out his otherwise lonely, solitary existence, you may find this simple act to be the highlight of your week.

- Consider that old wooden table in the basement that you use as a temporary workbench for sawing wood and doing household repairs. What if someone were to tell you it is a valuable antique? Instantly, your old worktable is transformed into a thing of value.

- Jokes are reframes. You are guided to think in one frame and then the frame – the meaning or context – changes. How many psychologists does it take to change a light bulb? Answer: Only one and the light bulb must want to change!

- Fairy tales often use reframes in the form of analogies or metaphors to help children see different perspectives or consequences.

- All metaphors assist us in seeing things from a different perspective.

- An excuse is a reframe that attributes a different meaning or context to your behaviors.

Here are some further notable examples of reframes:

- During the 1984 U.S. presidential campaign, there was considerable concern about Ronald Reagan's age. Speaking during the presidential debate with Walter Mondale, Reagan said, "I will not make age an issue of this campaign. I am not going to exploit, for political purposes, my opponent's youth and inexperience." Reagan's age was not an issue for the remainder of the campaign!

- There is a story about Thomas Watson, Sr., the first president of IBM. A young worker had made a mistake that lost IBM one million dollars in business. She was called in to the president's office for a discussion. As she walked in, she said, "Well, I guess you have called me here to fire me." "Fire you?" Mr. Watson replied. "I just spent a million dollars on your education!"

- A father brought his headstrong daughter to see Milton Erickson – the famous hypnotherapist. He said to Erickson, "My daughter doesn't listen to me or her mother. She is always expressing her own opinions." After the father finished describing his daughter's problem, Erickson replied, "Now isn't it good that she will be able to stand on her own two feet when she is ready to leave home?" The father sat in stunned silence. That was the extent of the therapy – the father now saw his daughter's opinionated behavior as a useful resource later in her life.

Content and context reframes

In NLP, there are two basic forms of reframes – *content* (or meaning) and *context* reframes.

Content reframe

What you choose to focus on determines the content or meaning of a situation. An electrical power failure may be viewed as disruptive, a major disaster, given all you have to accomplish. Alternatively, it may be viewed as an opportunity to spend some intimate time with your spouse, or to have fun with your children finding innovative ways to manage the situation.

A content reframe is useful for statements such as: "I get annoyed when my boss stands behind me while I am working." Notice how this situation is given a narrow, specific meaning – which may or may not be true – thus, the resourcefulness and possible courses of action are limited. To reframe this situation, remember the NLP presupposition, "every behavior has a positive intention" and ask questions such as:

- What other meaning could the boss's behavior have? Or, for what purpose does he do it? A possible reframe might be: "Is it possible he wants to help and does not know how to offer his assistance in any other way?"
- What is the positive value in this behavior? The positive value might be related to the boss's behavior or it might be related to the speaker's behavior. A possible reframe if you are the speaker's coach might be: "Isn't it great that you know your boundaries and are not prepared to allow someone to violate them?"

If you are experiencing a physical problem (including phobias and allergies), you may ask yourself, "Is this problem useful to me in some way?" For example, it may give you permission to say no to certain requests. If this is the case, you could ask yourself, "Is there some other way that I can get this same positive benefit without having to have the physical problem?"

Context reframe:

Almost all behaviors are useful or appropriate in some context. Interrupting a speaker by standing up and offering your view in the middle of her lecture may be judged as inappropriate. To do this same behavior at the end of the presentation in order to provide a different perspective may be welcomed by all present.

A context reframe is useful for statements such as: "I am too pushy" or "I wish I didn't always focus on what might go wrong." In this situation, you have assumed that this type of behavior has no value. You need to discover when it can be of value by asking yourself the question, "When or where would this behavior be useful or viewed as a resource?" Possible reframes for the two statements at the beginning of this paragraph might be: "Isn't that a great skill to have when you need to get things done?" or "Isn't that a great skill to have when you need to avoid potential problems?"

Children and parenting

Children exhibit all sorts of behaviors – some appropriate and some not so appropriate. Focusing mainly on a child's inappropriate behaviors may result in the child feeling overly criticized or attacked, which in turn may cause an increase in problem behavior or the child becoming defiant or defensive. As an alternative, a parent may choose two courses of action:

- Assuming every behavior has a positive intention, make an effort to discover that positive intention. You can then discuss with the child other behaviors that would meet both your needs and the child's. This is an example of a content reframe.
- You may point out where or in what context that type of behavior is acceptable, thus validating to the child that his behaviors are useful in certain contexts. This is an example of a context reframe.

Concluding thoughts

When presenting a reframe to another person:

- Make sure you have rapport and their permission to provide them with a different perspective (reframe).
- You may believe your reframe is the best ever and yet it may not work for the other person – simply because she has a different model of the world than you do. Remember the NLP presupposition that there is no failure, only feedback, and explore other possible reframes.
- If you present the reframe in the form of a question or a metaphor, it will most likely be considered more fully than if you present it as a statement of fact.
- Some NLP novices have a tendency to say they "reframed" someone. In fact, you can't reframe anyone other than yourself. The best you can do is to ask someone to consider your reframe and then he can choose whether it reframes his experience.

5.4. SLEIGHT OF MOUTH

Sleight of mouth is a very powerful set of reframing patterns for persuasion and conversational belief change. Coaches, those in the helping professions, managers and others can use them to assist their clients, staff or colleagues to look at their limiting beliefs from different perspectives. As a result, sleight of mouth patterns have the potential to shift the responsibility for a limiting belief back to the person who created it – putting him at cause and thus expanding his model of the world and providing him with more choices. These patterns were developed by Robert Dilts through modeling the verbal patterns of people such as Karl Marx, Milton Erickson, Abraham Lincoln, Jesus and Mohandas Gandhi. For more information on sleight of mouth, please see Robert Dilts' book *Sleight of Mouth: The Magic of Conversational Belief Change*, Meta Publications, 1999.

Taken out of context or viewed from certain perspectives, some sleight of mouth responses may seem very harsh or callous. This is not the intention. All reframing and sleight of mouth patterns should be used to support the client in expanding his model of the world so other possibilities may be considered. The value of any sleight of mouth response should be viewed in terms of whether it is helpful to the client.

Dilts identified fourteen different sleight of mouth patterns. For a particular intervention, you would not use all fourteen, but rather a subset that best supports your client. As you review the different patterns, you may discover that you have used each of them at one time or another to assist people in getting a different view of the world. It is useful to be comfortable generating a response using any of the fourteen patterns, as this will give you flexibility in responding to your client or others and not be locked into one or two favorites.

Beliefs

Beliefs define the relationship between values and their indicators, consequences and the type of activities that generate them. The belief that "good health results from exercise" links the value "good health" to the activity "exercise." Beliefs are often expressed in the form of a *complex equivalence* (A equals, is equivalent to, or means B) or a *cause–effect* (A causes (because), makes, leads to, produces, or results in B).

Sleight of mouth patterns work well for belief change. To use sleight of mouth patterns, the client's belief must be expressed in terms of a complex equivalence or cause–effect assertion. The statement, "I don't believe in reorganizing business units," does not reveal the full belief and gives us little to work with. To ascertain the person's full belief, you could ask questions such as: "What does reorganizing a business unit *mean* to you?" "What are the *consequences* of a business reorganization?" "What will a business reorganization *lead to*?" Your client needs to respond with a complex equivalence or cause–effect so you have something to work with.

Sleight of mouth patterns

To illustrate the sleight of mouth patterns, let's assume your client has a deeply held belief he states as: "Reorganizing this unit is irresponsible *because* it will lead to layoffs." This represents a legitimate belief, but one that can limit your client's options. This belief can be broken down into two parts: A *because* B (i.e. cause–effect assertion). A – reorganizing this unit is irresponsible, because B – it will lead to layoffs. In the following patterns, we can focus on either A or B or both. Only one example is given for each of the sleight of mouth patterns and many other examples are possible. The examples provided are in the context of a manager responding to an employee who has expressed the above belief.

1. **Intention:** What could be the positive intention?

   Possible positive intention: Security. Response: I very much admire and support your desire for security.

2. **Redefine:** Use words that are similar but may imply something different.

   Replace *irresponsible* with *careless* and *layoffs* with *unable to adjust*. Response: I agree that we must be careful of how this is undertaken so people can adjust to the new environment.

3. **Consequences:** Focus on a consequence that leads to challenging the belief.

   A consequence may be to "take responsibility." Response: Recognizing our respective responsibilities is a key step in mitigating the possibility of layoffs.

4. **Chunk down:** Look at a specific element that challenges the belief.

   Response: I'm not sure how proposing an organization chart that clearly describes staff roles and responsibilities would be construed as irresponsible.

5. **Chunk up:** Generalize in order to change the relationship defined by the belief.

   Response: Any change can have unforeseen consequences.

6. **Counter example:** Find an exception that challenges the generalization defined by the belief.

   Response: It is hard for me to see business reorganization as irresponsible when the last reorganization saved the company from insolvency.

7. **Analogy/metaphor:** Use an analogy or metaphor that challenges the generalization defined by the belief.

   Response: Good gardeners are always finding ways to re-energize the soil so plants have the nutrients and resources to grow strong and healthy.

8. **Apply to self:** Use key aspects of the belief to challenge the belief.

Response: Wouldn't it also be irresponsible and lead to layoffs if we do not do something different to resolve our current problems?

9. **Another outcome:** Propose a different outcome that challenges the relevancy of the belief.

Response: Perhaps the issue is not so much whether we reorganize, but whether we are doing the right things to maintain our jobs.

10. **Hierarchy of criteria:** Reassess the belief based on a more important criterion.

Response: Knowing how to act responsibly is more important than not taking any action at all.

11. **Change frame size:** Re-evaluate the implication of the belief in the context of a longer or shorter time frame, a larger number of people or an individual point of view, or from a larger or smaller perspective.

Response: Highly successful organizations have been restructuring to meet changing needs for centuries. Those that do not take these measures eventually disappear or are absorbed by other organizations.

12. **Meta frame:** Challenge the basis for the belief. For instance, formulate a theory about the origin of the belief.

Response: Is it possible you say this because you believe you do not have the skills to adjust to the change?

13. **Model of the world:** Look at the belief from a different perspective or model of the world.

Response: Are you aware that some people see a reorganization as an opportunity to learn new skills and assume more challenging duties?

14. **Reality strategy:** Reassess the belief with the knowledge that beliefs are based on specific perceptions.

Response: What particular aspects of the reorganization do you feel fearful about it?

5.5. STRATEGIES

A strategy is the means by which you organize your thoughts and behaviors to accomplish a specific outcome. A strategy is also known as a habit, process, plan, approach, procedure, pattern or program. Everything you do is based on a strategy, many of which are outside of your conscious awareness. You have strategies for being healthy, being depressed, being bored, problem solving, remembering/forgetting, falling in love, parenting, negotiating, being a leader, being angry, having fun, creating wealth, overeating, to name just a few.

Strategies reflect your beliefs and values and provide a context for your behaviors. A strategy always aims for a positive outcome – as viewed from the strategy owner's model of the world. From another person's perspective, the outcome may not be considered as positive. However, the strategy owner feels it is the best choice available given his view of the world and the resources he believes he has available.

An analogy

A common analogy for describing a strategy is that of baking a cake. The basic components for baking a cake are: ingredients (representational systems), the appropriate quantities and qualities of the ingredients (submodalities) and a specific order or series of steps. If the ingredients or quantities and qualities are changed, it is not the same cake. If the order is changed – adding the eggs after the cake has been baked – you have something very different.

A strategy is a recipe and has three crucial aspects:

- The sequence of the steps.
- The representational systems used.
- The distinctions within the representation systems – the submodalities.

Some strategies may play out over several weeks or months – for example, when buying a car; others, like becoming angry, may fire in the blink of an eye.

Motivation strategy

Each step in a strategy is one of the representational systems – something that you say to yourself (auditory digital), see, hear, feel, taste or smell. This can be either internal, as a memory or something you imagine in the future, or external. For example, part of my motivation strategy to write this section on strategies is as follows:

- I have a picture in my mind of the finished book (V^i)
- I see what I have written so far (V^e), and see in my mind that "strategies" is the next section (V^i)
- I say to myself (A^i_d) in a certain tonality (A^i), "I'm ready!" This is a synesthesia because both occur at the same time (A^i_d/A^i).
- I get a good feeling about writing this section (K^i).

In summary, my motivation strategy is $V^i \rightarrow V^e \rightarrow V^i \rightarrow A^i_d/A^i \rightarrow K^i$. Order is important and so are the submodalities of each step. My first picture is a big bright internal picture. If it were a small, dark internal picture, the rest of the strategy would not run as presented.

The previous paragraph describes my motivation strategy; yours may be similar or quite different. This is a very important point. Far too often people assume that the way they like to do something is the way that everyone else likes to do it. Good sales staff know that people have different buying habits and strategies. Poor sales staff assume that everyone likes to buy things the way they do. Teachers, managers and coaches cannot assume everyone likes to work or get motivated the same way that they do. We are all different with different approaches.

In NLP, we focus on the process and structure – the steps, the representational systems and associated submodalities – that produce specific results. We don't focus on the content or subject matter making up the various steps – what you actually see in the picture. Thus, it is possible to apply an effective strategy to a different context – for example, a creative strategy for designing furniture may be useful for designing houses – or a recognized expert's strategy may be used by someone else to assist her in achieving similar results.

Strategies within strategies

We have strategies within strategies, *sequential* strategies and *parallel* strategies. For example, suppose you are a manager negotiating a lease for office space. You have a strategy for this negotiation. Within the overall negotiation, you will have a strategy for how to respond to individual demands. This is called a *nested* strategy. Once the negotiation is completed, another strategy will kick in for getting the office space ready. Parallel to these two strategies, you will have a strategy for managing those who work for you. All of these strategies will be part of your overall management strategy.

How are strategies created?

From infancy onward, our primary way of learning is trial and error. We do something and consciously or unconsciously assess the feedback. Have we been punished or rewarded for our actions? If we feel we've been punished, we alter our strategies and do something different the next time. If we feel we've been rewarded, we internalize what we have done and run the program again and again – and a strategy is born. As we developed other strategies, they became organized together to make up our capabilities.

T.O.T.E. model

The T.O.T.E. model is an effort to describe how our brains work and was first presented by George A. Miller, Eugene Gallanter and Karl H. Pribram in their book, *Plans and the Structure of Behavior* (New York: Holt, Reinhart and Winston, 1960). T.O.T.E. stands for *Test-Operate-Test-Exit*.

The T.O.T.E. is a model only; we make no assertion that it is one hundred percent correct. However, it does give us a useful way to look at strategies, understand how they work and how they can be changed if we are not getting the results we desire.

The first test, often called a *trigger*, begins the strategy. In the test phase, you establish a representation of the desired state or outcome and criteria that can be used to assess your progress. You then feed the criteria forward to the second test as a method of assessing if your outcome has been achieved. Without specific criteria, the process will loop with no exit possible – paralysis by analysis.

Operation is what you do to achieve your outcome: the gathering, accessing or creation of data – make a picture in your mind, talk to yourself, gather facts and figures, listen and absorb, and so on.

The second *test* compares the information you have gathered during the operation phase with the criteria that were fed forward from the first test. If the criteria have been satisfied, then you *exit* and manifest the outcome. If the criteria are not satisfied, you can revisit the operation phase for more information or change the criteria and thus the outcome. You again revisit the operation phase or exit, depending upon whether the new criteria have been satisfied.

The exit (sometimes called a *choice point*) represents the outcome of the second test.

To illustrate the T.O.T.E. model, consider the following: Trigger – I need a new car. I first decide on the following criteria: brand new, black, convertible BMW for US$35,000. Operation – I visit car dealerships, search the Internet and read classified ads to gather information. Test – I compare the information that I gathered with my criteria. Exit – If my criteria are satisfied, I purchase the car. If my criteria are not satisfied, I may decide that my search was not extensive enough. So, maintaining the same criteria, I do more research (revisit the operation phase) or I change the criteria (and outcome) on the basis of the information I have gathered, which may result in deciding not to purchase this particular car at this time.

T.O.T.E. model observations

- The trigger is what starts the strategy in motion. If there is something that I would like to achieve, but the trigger never gets fired, clearly I will not achieve that outcome. On the other hand, if the outcome from a strategy is undesirable (excessive eating, for example) and the trigger for this strategy is removed, this outcome will not be achieved either.

- The operation phase is a series of steps to gather, access or create information. If this process is interrupted in some way – just like removing one or more lines from a computer program – the process cannot be completed as originally planned, and some other outcome will result. This is called a *pattern interrupt*. For example:

o Have you ever watched very young children as they begin to cry because they were told they could not do something? This is a process or strategy that occurs over at least a minute. First they begin to pout and their lower lip begins to swell. As soon as their criteria for crying are satisfied, they cry. When my children were this age and I noticed this process beginning, I would make a funny face or noise to interrupt them. This would distract them and cause them to laugh, until they remembered that they were running the strategy for crying and begin to pout again. I would then make another funny face or sound, causing them to laugh and interrupting their strategy. After a few repetitions, we would reach a point where I no longer needed to do anything. As soon as they began to pout, they would laugh. We had created a new strategy – an association between pouting and laughing.

o Remember that the operation phase comprises a number of steps, each based on a representational system, and each of which has specific submodalities. If one of the steps involves a big, bright picture, and we change this to a small dark picture, we have changed the process and, most likely, the outcome that was originally planned will not be achieved.

o NLP has been known for its fast phobia cures. One such cure for spiders or snakes is based on changing the size submodality. Once your client feels safe (for instance, behind a piece of imaginary Plexiglas), have her imagine, at a comfortable distance, a picture of a spider on the other side of the Plexiglas. Gradually, have her make the picture larger – size of a quarter, chair, table, room, house and city. At some point the picture becomes ridiculous and the client will simply smile or laugh. You have just destroyed part of the process and it will not work as it did in the past.

• If there are no criteria or they are not clear, an assessment as to whether the process should exit cannot be made and the person will continually cycle through the test/operation phases. She may feel stuck or confused and need outside assistance to move on.

• Effective performance comes from 1) having a clear representation of the desired outcome, 2) sensory evidence to provide feedback in order to accurately determine progress toward the outcome, 3) a variety of operations to reach the outcome, and 4) the behavior flexibility to implement these choices.

Elicitation, utilization, design and installation

There are four ways to work with strategies:

- Elicitation: Discover a person's strategy – the sequence of steps, along with their attributes.
- Utilization: Use the elicited sequence of steps to influence the person's response. Or, take the key components of an effective strategy and apply in a different context.
- Design or change: Create a strategy to achieve a specific outcome for which no strategy exists or for which the current strategy is ineffective or inefficient.
- Installation: Install a new strategy to achieve a specific outcome.

Elicitation

Elicitation involves defining or modeling a person's particular mental steps in performing or accomplishing some task. That is, you need to determine three crucial aspects: 1) the sequence of the steps, 2) the representational systems used, and 3) the distinctions within the representational systems – the submodalities.

A strategy may be elicited for the following reasons:

- As part of a modeling exercise to obtain the strategy of an expert – how does she do it?
- To be able to influence a person's response. A salesman will have greater success if he supports his client in buying according to her strategy.
- To determine how an ineffective or inefficient strategy can be improved.

To elicit a person's strategy, either have them recall a specific event (from start to finish) or have them carry out the task. As they do, ask lots of questions, using the meta model to gain clarification, listening for predicates and watching eye accessing cues. You may have them recall or redo the task several times before you have clearly identified the sequence of the steps, representational systems and submodalities.

Why do we use the meta model, predicates and eye accessing cues? Many patterns of behavior are characterized by *unconscious competence*. That is, we are not aware of all the mental operations we go through as part of our strategy. We focus on what we are doing, and not on the subtle mental processes by which we select and guide our actions. Clarifications via the meta model and observing sensory-specific language patterns and eye accessing cues help to identify the specific steps of the strategy.

Strategies originate from several key beliefs, values and assumptions. Thus, elicitation must also involve identifying those beliefs on which a particular strategy is based. For example, the basis for my strategies during NLP practitioner training is my belief that people have all the resources they need to resolve their issues. Hence my strategies focus on creating a place of safety and asking appropriate and respectful questions that will assist participants in clarifying their issues, discovering the resources they have and identifying the steps that can be taken.

Utilization

Once you have elicited a person's strategy, you can utilize it to influence or direct that person's responses. For instance, when you present something to your boss for a decision, pace or match his decision-making strategy.

On the other hand, you can take an effective strategy from one context to improve similar strategies in other contexts. Let's suppose I am very creative when it comes to music composition, but lacking creativity at work. As my coach, you could elicit both strategies, notice the key differences and then assist me in *mapping across* key aspects of my music strategy to the strategy I use at work. Mapping across requires the use of one or more of the techniques presented under Installation, which is described in more detail on the following page. Comparing the two strategies for similarities and differences is called *contrastive analysis*. I have used this approach with students who obtain As in some subjects and Ds and Fs in other subjects to discover the differences in their strategies. Once they became consciously aware of the difference, most simply chose to implement the more successful strategy.

Design

Sometimes new strategies need to be designed to fix an ineffective strategy or to achieve a particular task. Strategy design involves identifying the sequence of representational steps that will most effectively accomplish a particular task or reach a particular outcome.

A strategy can be either an asset or a limitation. Often we outgrow a strategy, but neglect to change it to suit the new situation. For example, a strategy that you used when you were eight years old to get what you wanted from your parents may not be effective with your parents, spouse or boss when you are an adult. Yet how many of us unconsciously carry these strategies into adulthood? Strategy design is about continually optimizing and updating our strategies. As parents, we need to modify our strategies for interacting with our children as they become mature adults.

For strategies to be efficient and effective, they should be functionally and structurally well-formed. A strategy is functionally well-formed (based on the T.O.T.E. model), if there is:

- A trigger that starts the process and establishes the final criteria and a well-defined representation of the outcome.
- An operational phase that uses all three major representational systems – each representational system provides information that may not be available from the other representational systems – with several different paths available to bring the present state closer to the desired state. If there is only one path and something is blocking this path, then the strategy will not complete.
- A test phase that compares the information gathered during the operational phase to the criteria established for the desired state. This should include external checks. Without an external check, you get mired in your own internal experiences.
- A decision – an exit point that determines the next step.

Installation

The more popular ways to install a strategy are:

- Metaphor. A story that has the desired sequence of steps, representational systems and submodalities. Fairy tales are metaphors and often result in children choosing a different strategy and hence manifesting different behaviours (e.g., *The Boy Who Cried Wolf*).
- Rehearsing. You can rehearse in your mind by going through all of the steps or you can actually go through the steps with some friends playing key roles in the strategy. Rehearse until it becomes a way of life.
- Reframing. This can be used to provide you with a different perspective on your current strategy, thus showing how it can be modified to achieve the outcomes you desire.
- Anchoring. Chaining anchors can be used. Anchor each step (with representational systems and submodalities) to separate knuckles, then chain these anchors together.

Spelling strategy

Many people have difficulty spelling; this is usually the result of using an ineffective strategy. In school, we are often taught to sound out the word before spelling it. This strategy, based on phonics, is ineffective. In fact, if we use phonics to spell the word *phonics*, it comes out as *fonix*. Other people, who have had a bad experience with spelling, recall their past feelings of failure and embarrassment when asked to spell a word, hence they are unable to access the resources required to complete the task. Robert Dilts modeled the strategies of successful spellers and created a visual spelling strategy that works well for poor spellers and those diagnosed as learning disabled or dyslexic.

The basis of the following spelling strategy is the work of Robert Dilts and Todd Epstein, *Dynamic Learning,* (Meta Publications, 1995).

1. Divide the word into syllables and write it on a piece of paper. For example, Al-bu-quer-que.

2. Hold the paper in your visual remembered quadrant – up and to the left for most people (see chapter 3.3 – Eye accessing cues).

3. Close your eyes and think of a time when you were confident and relaxed. When the feeling is strong, open your eyes and look at the correct spelling.

4. Remove the paper and keep your eyes in the visual remembered quadrant and continue to see the correct spelling in your mind's eye.

5. While looking at the mental image, spell the word, one syllable at a time.

6. If you have difficulty, return to step two.

7. Looking at the mental image in the visual remembered quadrant, spell the word backward. If you have difficulty, return to step two. The purpose of spelling the word backward is to verify that you are indeed using a visual image. If you can spell the word backward, you can certainly spell it forward.

The Disney strategy for creativity

In his book, *Strategies of Genius* (Volumes I, II and II, Meta Publications, 1994–5), Robert Dilts has elicited the thought strategies of Aristotle, Sherlock Holmes, Walt Disney, Wolfgang Amadeus Mozart, Albert Einstein, Sigmund Freud, Leonardo da Vinci and Nikola Tesla. This section describes a creativity strategy based on an approach used by Walt Disney, as elicited by Robert Dilts.

When working on a new project, Disney used three distinct perspectives – those of a dreamer, a realist, and a critic – and had rules on when and how the different perspectives interacted with each other. He would encourage his team to participate in these perspectives along with him and would create an environment that encouraged each perspective at the appropriate time.

Each of the three distinct perspectives represents a whole thinking strategy on its own:

The Dreamer:
• Vision: The big picture; anything is possible.

The Realist:
• Action: Viewed from first position – fully associated (see chapter 4.2). What does it feel like to be part of this dream? Act as if the dream is possible and develop a plan to realistically reach the dream.

The Critic:
• Logic: Viewed from second position (fully dissociated from any ownership

of the dream). As a recipient or consumer of the final product, what is your reaction? What are the risks? Ensure quality and avoid problems by looking at the proposed plan under various "what if" scenarios.

Disney had a very clean and distinct separation between these perspectives. He insisted that each be completed before going to the next one. For each perspective, he used different locations and often included different people for the discussions.

Exercise: The Disney planning strategy for individuals or teams
If you are the head of a team who needs to establish a successful plan for your current project, the Disney planning strategy will ensure that you achieve your outcome. The following steps are a guideline:

1. Select three distinctly different physical locations and label them Dreamer, Realist and Critic. If possible, you can even decorate the space accordingly.

2. Anchor the appropriate strategy to each physical location, and make sure you break state in between. For each strategy, use these techniques:

   a. Dreamer: Recall a time when you were able to creatively dream up new ideas without any limitations. Anchor this to the first location. If possible, also take on the physiology of a dreamer – perhaps leaning back gazing at the sky – during the anchoring process.

   b. Realist: Recall a time when you were able to think very realistically and were able to develop a plan to put your ideas into action. Anchor this to the second location. If possible, also take on the appropriate physiology during the anchoring process.

   c. Critic: Recall a time when you were able to identify key problems and provide constructive criticism. Anchor this to the third location. If possible, also take on the appropriate physiology during the anchoring process.

3. Pick an outcome that you wish to achieve. Physically step into the Dreamer location and assume the appropriate physiology. See yourself accomplishing the outcome and think about it in a free and unrestricted manner. Identify the benefits. You may wish to answer the following questions:

   • What do you want to achieve?

   • For what purpose?

   • What are the benefits and how will you know when you have achieved them?

- When will the benefits occur?

- What will this outcome lead to?

- Who will you be when you achieve this outcome?

Once this is fully complete, step out of this location and break state.

4. Step into the Realist location and assume the appropriate physiology. Associate fully into the dream and develop a course of action for achieving the dream (including time frames, milestones and resources). You may wish to answer the following questions:

   - How will the outcome be achieved?

   - How will you measure progress and know when you have achieved the outcome?

   - What resources do you need, what are the key outputs and time frames?

   - Where will it be done?

   - Are all the steps necessary? Are some missing?

   Once this is fully complete, step out of this location and break state.

5. Step into the Critic location and assume the appropriate physiology. Make sure the proposal is ecological. Identify potential problems and phrase criticisms as questions for the dreamer – criticize the dream, not the dreamer. The following questions may provide you with guidelines:

   - Will the plan assist you in achieving the outcome?

   - Who will be affected by this outcome? What are their needs, concerns and expectations? Why might they object?

   - What are the benefits of the status quo and which should be maintained?

   - Are there times and places that should be avoided?

   - What's missing from the plan?

   - What could stop this outcome from being achieved?

   Once this is fully complete, step out of this location and break state.

6. Step into the Dreamer location and assume the appropriate physiology. Creatively develop solutions to the questions and problems raised by the Critic.

7. Continue to revisit steps four, five and six until all three positions support your outcome and plan.

5.6. MODELING

We are continually adjusting to our surroundings by observing others whom we perceive to be good at what they do and engaging in similar behaviors. As young children, this is how we learned to walk and talk, and we continue to do it into adulthood by mimicking the behaviors, dress or speech patterns of people we admire and respect. This form of learning is called *modeling*. Sometimes when we see the effects of certain parental or teaching behaviors, we choose to adopt or model the exact opposite behaviors in order not to create similar results in others – especially our children.

In the early 1970s, NLP began with Richard Bandler and John Grinder modeling the language and behavior patterns of known experts such as Fritz Perls (gestalt therapy), Virginia Satir (family therapy) and Milton Erickson (hypnosis). Today, by modeling people with noteworthy or exceptional abilities, the NLP body of knowledge continues to be developed and improved. There are many newly discovered patterns, skills and techniques. These are being used increasingly in counseling, coaching, education and business for more effective communication, personal development and accelerated learning.

Most people who are good at what they do are not consciously aware of how they do it – it just "comes naturally." It is therefore the responsibility of the person doing the modeling to observe and ask questions in order to identify the essential elements of thinking and behavior and to make these available for others to use.

Often, when we think of modeling, we imagine people who are good at communication, training, sales, managing, or who are perhaps involved in sports, social services or helping others. Steve and Connirae Andreas have taken a slightly different approach. They first model the problem and its resolution separately, and then model a process that makes the transition from one to the other. Using this technique, they have developed patterns to assist people in addressing grief, guilt, shame and forgiveness. Some modeling projects are undertaken in days, whereas others can take as long as two years, as was the case when Penny Tompkins and James Lawley modeled David Grove's questioning technique called *clean language*. (James Lawley and Penny Tompkins, *Metaphors in Mind: Transformation through Symbolic Modelling*, The Developing Company Press, 2000).

An often-used form of modeling is through mentoring. However, the mentor may not often be consciously aware of his critical beliefs, skills and strategies or how he uses them to be successful. If the person being mentored does not know how to model this expert, then he does not get full value from the experience.

Modeling is more than observing behaviors

Many people model someone they admire by observing and adopting their behaviors. Modeling in NLP, however, takes this technique to a higher level. Through observation and questioning, you need to become aware of how your expert filters information (beliefs, values, meta programs), their use of language patterns and tonality and their thought processes at each of the logical levels.

For the logical levels, as you observe your expert, you may wish to explore each of the following and notice how the answers the expert provides at each level are interlinked:

- Environment. (Where, when, with whom?) Is there a specific context in which your expert applies this skill?

- Behavior. (What?) What are your expert's key behaviors?

- Capabilities/strategies. (How?) Elicit the expert's strategies. Are any particularly relevant skills required?

- Beliefs and values. (Why?) What does the expert believe about themselves, and about other people? What does the expert value?

- Identity. (Who?) What is the role, mission or identity assumed by the expert?

- Spirituality. (Who else?) What is the expert's purpose or connection with the larger system?

The modeling process

The following process is based on the work of Robert Dilts:

1. Identify the context and the skill that you wish to model.

   Chunk this down to a reasonable size. Sometimes it is more effective to model a number of small chunks and then integrate these into a larger model.

   The skill you model may not be transferable to other contexts. For example, if you model someone who excels at business presentations, this skill may not be transferable to giving presentations to children in daycare.

2. Find one or more people whom you consider to be excellent at the skill you wish to model.

   Modeling more than one person allows you to separate what is essential from what is idiosyncratic. If you are modeling one person, you may wish to observe them performing this skill in at least three different situations.

3. Gather information. Determine the critical factors for:

- Language patterns and tonality – meta model, Milton model and predicates.
- Physiology.
- Meta programs.
- Each of the logical levels.

This can be done in a variety of ways.

- Observe your "expert" demonstrating the skill. Notice eye movements for potential clues. If possible, ask your expert questions as she demonstrates the skill in order to determine her thought processes, strategies, beliefs and values. If you cannot question your expert as she demonstrates the skill, ask her questions afterward.

- Use perceptual positions. If the skill has an impact on others, experience this impact yourself – from first position – and gain insights into what your expert is doing to create this result. From second position, adopt her physiology, use of language and perspective to gain insights into her beliefs, values and strategies. Take what you have learned from these two positions and notice if you can reproduce the results obtained by your expert. Use third position to notice any differences between your approach and that of the expert and the results that are obtained from each approach. Use fourth position to observe any differences between your approach and your expert's on the overall system.

4. Identify the critical factors that all your experts had in common or that were present in each of the different situations.

5. By taking away one factor at a time, determine the minimum number of factors required to achieve the desired result.

   You can also identify the variability of each factor by noticing how much you can vary it and still achieve the desired result.

6. Organize the information you have gathered into a logical, coherent structure or "model."

7. Test the effectiveness and usefulness of your model in various contexts and situations, making sure the desired results are achieved.

8. Design a process to transfer your model to others who can use it.

5.7. VALUES

Values are principles, standards or qualities that we consider to be worthwhile, important or desirable. They are the reason why we are motivated to do things. Values most often operate at an unconscious level – deep inside – as the core or purpose in our lives. We either move toward what we value or move away from what we do not value. Many people refer to this as moving toward pleasure and away from pain. When observing other people, we may be surprised to see them moving toward something that we do not value. However, in their model of the world, they see what they are moving toward as valuable.

Included in values are important but intangible criteria such as success, integrity, spirituality, praise, honesty, safety, and so on. These highly valued criteria, which are often expressed as nominalizations, serve as a focal point around which our beliefs are organized. As we go through our daily lives, some of us focus on these intangible criteria, while others focus on tangible values such as money or possessions. However, behind the material values the intangible criteria still exist, and can be determined by chunking up – asking the question, "For what purpose?"

Few of us are consciously aware of our values. We tend to go through much of our lives on autopilot. Most of our values were established very early on. The values that made sense and served us well in our youth may still be driving our behaviors years later, simply because we are not aware of them and have not changed them to meet our current needs. Becoming consciously aware of our values can give us insight into why we pursue certain things or behave in certain ways. This awareness can also provide the opportunity to assess whether these values truly reflect who we are today, or whether they are values others have imposed on us.

As we mature, our values and their meanings change. Safety as a child may have meant not upsetting mommy or daddy. Does it still mean the same thing today? As adults, we need to reassess our values and likely make different choices from the more mature perspective.

Values also have a hierarchy or order of importance that affects how we experience the world and live our lives. A person who values health more than a successful career will live a different life than one who places a higher value on a successful career.

Values and emotions

One of the easiest ways to discover your values is to look behind what is driving your emotions. For example:

- Anger. You become angry because you or someone else has violated something you value.
- Happy. You are happy because something you value is being achieved.

- Excited. You are excited because something you value has the potential of being achieved.
- Guilt. You feel guilty because you have violated one of your values and you want to avoid doing it again.
- Sad. You are sad because something you value is not available to you.
- Fear. You are fearful of losing something you value or having it violated.

Of course, there are many other emotions. Think about some of the emotions you have recently experienced, and become curious about exploring the values behind those emotions.

Reassessing and aligning your values

Having knowledge of our values and their order of importance allows us to be more in control of our behaviors. We are then able to consciously make choices that support who we truly are rather than living life on autopilot. As well, the priority we have assigned to values may be out of date or inferred – incorrectly – through the perceived wishes of others. If you are coaching, the following exercise provides a process for your client to become consciously aware of his values and to align them in support of his aspirations.

1. Ask your client to decide on a context that is important to him: life, career, family or relationships, for example.

2. Have your client list his values. Ensure that your client recognizes they are his own values and not those that he thinks others expect of him. Also, make sure he expresses his values positively, i.e., "healthy" rather than "avoiding poor health." Your goal in step two is to uncover all the values your client considers to be important within the context he has selected.

    a. Have your client get comfortable. For the context selected in step one, ask your client, "What is important to you?" and "What motivates you?" The first five to seven values listed will reflect the surface structure – those values he is consciously aware of. However, you want your client to probe more deeply inside himself to become aware of those values that are operating at an unconscious level. To do this, ask him at least two more times what else is important to him or motivates him. Continue until no new values come to mind.

    b. Ask your client to think of times he was happy, sad or angry, and to notice the values behind those emotions.

    c. Have your client pick the top ten values from (a) and (b). Then, for each of these values, ask him, "For what purpose?" or "How would you know if you have achieved it?" If additional values are discovered, add these to the list.

   d. Show your client the list of values elicited and ask:

      i.   If you had all of these values satisfied, is there anything that could happen that would make you leave your life, career or relationship – i.e., the context in step one?

      ii. What would have to be true for you to stay if (i) occurred – that is, if something caused you to want to leave your life, career or relationship? What would be important enough to override (i)?

      iii. Given (i) and (ii) are true, is there something else that would cause you to want to leave?

      iv. Repeat (ii) and (iii) until your client cannot think of any other reasons for staying or leaving.

3.   Have your client group all the similar values under acceptable titles. For instance, your client may have identified friendship and companionship as important values. When he reviews them, he may consider them similar enough to be grouped under the title of "friendship."

4.   Ask your client to identify his top ten values from all of those listed in steps two and three and put them in order of importance (the first being most important and the last, the least important) – as he lives his life today.

5.   Identify potential conflicts. Have a conversation with your client about his top ten values and listen for potential conflicts between these ten values or with other values not in the top ten. These conflicts may result in a value being ranked much lower than expected. Examples of possible conflicts are:

    • Financial security and freedom. Your client may feel that working to achieve financial security will mean giving up his freedom.

    • Intimacy and safety. Your client may feel he cannot feel safe and at the same time be intimate with another person.

6.   Resolve potential conflicts. Parts integration is often used (more about this technique in chapter 6.6). Conflicts can also be resolved by reframing, timeline (chapter 6.2) and other techniques.

7.   Once the conflicts have been resolved, have your client review the top ten values and make any final adjustments to the order.

8. Verify the order of the first five values using two-by-two comparisons as follows:

   a. Have your client compare the first-ranked value with the second-ranked value. Ask him, "If you could only have one of these, which one would you choose?"

      i. If he selects the second, then replace one with two and go to step (b).

      ii. If he selects the first, then go to step (b).

   b. Now compare item one with item three, then one with four, then one with five, following the process in (i) and (ii) above.

   c. Once you have clearly identified the top value, go on to verify the second most important value by comparing item two with item three, then two with four, then two with five.

   d. Continue until you have verified the rankings of the five most important values.

   We work with only the top five values – the other values will have little influence – with the first-ranked value having the most influence. At this point, your client may be surprised that a value he thought was important did not make the top five.

9. Have your client look at the top five values and ask him if the top five values meet his needs and if the order is fully acceptable for how he would like to live his life.

   He may agree, in which case go to step ten. Or he may say, for example, that he would like to see health, which is ranked as number eight, figure in more prominently and be moved to number three. This may be easy for him to say, yet internally he may "see" health as number eight. You need to change how he stores the concept of health. This is done through submodalities (see chapter 5.1). If your client wishes health to be number three, then elicit the submodalities of the value that is ranked number two. Change the submodalities of health to those just elicited for the second most important value. Since we will not have elicited every submodality for the second most important value, health will move up the list and fall just short of the second most important value and be placed as number three.

10. Your client has now aligned and installed his five most important values according to how he wishes to live his life. Check the ecology (throughout the whole process), test and future pace.

Aligning values in your team/family

Not surprisingly, people operate from different values and have different interpretations of values. For example, I may value success and interpret it as people on the team working in harmony. You, on the other hand, may view success as completing the team project on time and respecting schedules and deadlines. In this situation, each of us may feel that the other person fully understands and supports our interpretation of success, until there is a critical deadline for completing a specific task. Only then do our values and interpretations come into conflict.

To manage diversity and minimize potential value conflicts in a team or family, everyone involved must recognize and understand that people have different values and interpretations of these values. Clarifying other people's values is an important part of mediation, negotiation, team building and effective communication.

The above exercise can be modified to work with teams, families or other groups. Members learn to commit to a shared value structure and have clarity on the meaning of those values. Values and how they are interpreted establish the motivation and culture of the group or system. Dysfunctional systems result from conflicts in basic values.

5.8. BELIEFS

Beliefs are views, guiding principles, judgments and decisions about ourselves, people close to us, our community and how the world functions. Your beliefs filter what you see, hear and feel in the world around you and as a result determine the meaning you associate with an event. Beliefs act as self-fulfilling prophecies. Your beliefs, whether they are limiting or empowering, determine your actions, which in turn verify your beliefs to be true. Over time, as you generate more evidence, your beliefs become increasingly entrenched and more real.

Beliefs operate at the "deep structure" level and influence the "surface structure" of our thoughts and behaviors. While we are aware of many of our beliefs, in general, our most influential beliefs operate outside of our conscious awareness. There are some beliefs that we view as absolute truths and never question – "that is just the way the world is!" A change in our beliefs can have a major impact on how we live our lives and the behaviors we manifest.

Once we believe in something, we tend to ignore counter-examples and accept only those events that reinforce that belief.

> If you believe you can or
> believe you can't, you're right.
>
> *–Henry Ford*

Beliefs can have a significant effect on your life, particularly your health. In their book *NLP and Health*, (Thorsons, 1996), Ian McDermott and Joseph O'Connor illustrate this very well with numerous references to medical cases. For example, in a typical clinical situation, about thirty-five percent of all cases receive as much pain relief from a placebo as from morphine – simply because the recipients believe it will work.

Do your beliefs limit you?

At one time, most people believed the world was flat, and there may still be some today who believe this. To verify this belief, just look at the ground below you – it's flat. In the distance you may see a few hills and valleys, but these are just ripples on an otherwise flat surface. All of the land is bounded by water and it is well known that if you sail far enough, you will fall off the edge of the world. This is certainly verified by those sailors who set sail and never return. For those who do return, they just didn't sail far enough.

In its time, this flat-world belief was very useful in explaining and predicting phenomena in a very localized area and most importantly, it kept people comfortable and safe. However, by encouraging people not to venture too far, it was also very limiting. In the preceding paragraph, notice how the belief can be used to explain certain occurrences and in so doing prove its own validity.

For society to advance, it was necessary for brave souls such as Christopher Columbus to challenge this belief and put his life, as he knew it, at risk. Thanks to Columbus, we were able to let go of the limiting belief of a flat world and explore other possibilities that eventually led us to entertain new and more expansive scientific theories (beliefs) of planets and galaxies, which future generations may view as equally limiting as the flat-world belief.

Do you have "flat-world" beliefs that keep you comfortable and safe and that prevent you from exploring your true potential? Do you choose to acknowledge only those events that are predicted by your limiting beliefs and then use these observations as proof that your limiting beliefs are indeed true? Is it time to step out of your comfort zone and set sail into the unknown? To push the boundaries of what you think you know and discover new lands and opportunities – a new reality?

Where do our beliefs come from?

Most of our beliefs originate from the time we were children. They are not based on fact, but on our perception of events at the time they were formed. We modeled people who played a significant role in our lives – parents, teachers, religious leaders, older siblings. We made generalizations based on single traumatic experiences or through trial and error, accepting those beliefs that brought us pleasure, avoided pain or provided safety. We accepted what we were told about ourselves – "you are stupid and incompetent" or "you can achieve whatever you choose."

Many of our limiting beliefs are based on misinterpretations of past events. As children, we did not have all of the resources we have today nor an awareness of all the facts. If we were mistreated by our parents or others, we very likely took things personally and erroneously accepted responsibility for their actions, assuming that it was *our* actions that created the situation. By accepting responsibility and not wishing to recreate a similar experience, we would vow, "I'll never do that again," thus limiting our self-expression and what is possible.

To illustrate how easy it is to establish a core belief, consider how elephants are trained. You often see elephants restrained by only a light rope and stake. Why is it that these massive animals don't just walk away, since they could easily break the rope or pull out the stake? Simply, they have been conditioned to accept that they cannot. If they had the ability to reason, we would simply say they believe they cannot!

When elephants are young, they are tied up with a very heavy rope and stake that they are unable to budge or break. After many futile attempts, they accept that no matter what they do, they cannot break free. Although not real, this limitation restricts their mobility, even in the face of danger.

Just as the elephants have done, what boundaries did you accept when you were a child that now limit how you live your life – and therefore your dreams and aspirations?

Changing beliefs

The first step to changing a belief is to become consciously aware of the belief and its impact on your life. Beliefs can be changed in a number of ways:

- We change or modify beliefs all the time as we receive and assess new information.

  At one time, you may have believed in Santa Claus – a very powerful belief that had a major impact on your behaviors around Christmas time. People may even have taken advantage of your belief to encourage you to behave in certain ways or "Santa won't come."

  Assuming you are not still holding steadfastly to this belief, how did you change it? I would imagine that you gathered information from your friends and parents and gradually questioned the belief until you realized that you could let it go and still get the positive benefits (gifts) and avoid the negative ones – perhaps the teasing of your friends.

- You can also install a new belief by simply choosing it, consciously following it, and noticing its positive effects until it becomes a way of life. At first, you may find it difficult to achieve the results you want. However, if you stick with it, you will find that it becomes easier and your performance improves. Following are the steps you can undertake to begin changing your beliefs:

  1. Become aware of your beliefs by making a list of your thoughts – the ones that are positive and support you in achieving your higher purpose. Make a separate list of the ones that don't support you.

  2. Identify the supporting and limiting beliefs behind these thoughts.

  3. Ask yourself, "What kind of world are these limiting beliefs creating for me?" Imagine what your life will be like, one, five and ten years from now if you continue to let these limiting beliefs determine your life.

  4. Turn these limiting, non-supporting beliefs into positive supporting beliefs.

  5. Each day, repeat these new beliefs to yourself several times and look for situations that reinforce them. Ignore those situations that don't reinforce these beliefs – after all, you have been ignoring the ones that are positive, so now it's time to ignore the ones that are negative.

- Reframing and sleight of mouth can be used to soften up a limiting belief and open the possibility of other choices.

- Timeline can be used to go back in time to a past memory that was significant in forming the limiting belief and reassessing it from the knowledge and capabilities you have as a fully functioning adult. Once this past memory is reassessed, there may be no basis for the limiting belief. With the new interpretation, the limiting belief can be let go and replaced by a more empowering belief.

- Submodalities can be used to change a limiting belief as follows (break state after each elicitation of the submodalities):

  1. Elicit the submodalities of the limiting belief.

  2. Elicit the submodalities of a belief that you used to hold, but is no longer true. For example, at one time you may have believed that you could not drive a car; today, that belief is no longer true.

3. Thinking about the limiting belief, change its submodalities to those of the belief that is no longer true.

4. Test and future pace.

5. Now replace the limiting belief with a new belief that you wish to hold. When this new belief is first stated, it is only a series of words. These are words you wish to install as a belief that influences how you live your life.

6. Elicit the submodalities of a belief that for you is true. For instance, you may have a belief that no matter what you have in the kitchen cupboard and refrigerator, you can make a meal that others will enjoy. Or no matter what is wrong with a car engine, you can fix it.

7. Think of your new belief, and change its submodalities to those of the belief that is true.

8. Test and future pace.

- In *NLP and Health* (Thorsons, 1996), Ian McDermott and Joseph O'Connor outline other approaches to changing beliefs. Robert Dilts has written extensively on this subject; his work can be found in the *Encyclopedia of Systemic NLP and NLP New Coding* (NLP University Press, 2000).

6.

Freeing Yourself from the Past

6.1. CHANGING YOUR PERSONAL HISTORY

Your memories form the basis of your thoughts in the present; at the same time, they also create your future. How useful is it, then, to continue to penalize yourself in the present and future because someone hurt you in the past? Yet many of us do exactly that. Are you hanging on to old hurts, and carrying them forward, jeopardizing both your present and your future? As children – and often as adults – we often unconsciously take responsibility for the actions of someone else. Is it not time to let go of childhood memories, and create a more compelling future for yourself?

In addition, have you ever misinterpreted an event or conversation simply because you did not have complete knowledge of the circumstances? As a child, you determined your feelings and views of life by observing and copying the behaviors of the adults around you, while not having complete knowledge of the pressures faced by these adults or their personal limitations. With this as your frame of reference, is it not possible that you may have *misinterpreted the past*? You cannot change what actually happened. You are, however, in charge of your memories; hence, you can reassess the past and use it as a resource rather than a limitation.

Many NLP techniques give you the opportunity to change your personal history by adding new resources to the "younger you" in a past memory or by reassessing a past memory with all of the resources and understanding of the adult you are today.

6.2. TIMELINES

The Merriam-Webster Online Dictionary defines time as "a nonspatial continuum that is measured in terms of events that succeed one another from past through present to future." This continuum allows us to distinguish between events that happened last year, yesterday, presently occurring, next week or next month.

In NLP, we call this continuum a *timeline*. The word timeline can be misunderstood. Some people, when they hear this term, think of the time continuum as linear – a line, and some think of it as a straight line (in school, it could not be just any line, but a straight line). Some people find that their timeline is indeed a line or a straight line; others find something quite different. Despite the differences, there is always a continuum. As an example, a participant in one of my classes had a timeline that was a sequence of clouds. She could easily distinguish which cloud was further in the past or future and, within a cloud, she could place events at different times.

Determining your timeline

Your unconscious mind maintains your timeline. In the following two methods for determining your timeline, it is important for you to be relaxed, fully open to any answer and accepting of the first thing that comes to mind. Bear in mind that all answers are correct, and if you start to analyze your answers and have an internal debate about your timeline, this is your conscious mind at work.

Method 1:
1. Make yourself comfortable, close your eyes and allow your unconscious mind to do all the work.

2. With your real or imaginary hand, point to the direction of your past and go with the first inclination or impulse you feel. You may feel inclined to point behind you, in front of you, to one side, or up or down.

3. With your real or imaginary hand, point to the direction of your future, going with your first inclination.

Method 2:
1. Make yourself comfortable, close your eyes and allow your unconscious mind to do all of the work.

2. Think of something that happened last week. As you do, notice the direction that the memory seemed to come from.

3. Repeat step two, replacing last week with last month, last year or several years ago.

4.   Now think of something that will happen next week. As you do, notice the direction that the memory seemed to come from.

5.   Repeat step four, replacing next week with next month, next year, and several years from now.

For both methods, notice that this arrangement implies a continuum of your memories from the past to the present and into the future. Notice if this continuum passes through your body (with the present inside your body) or if the continuum passes outside of your body.

Through time and in time

The form of your timeline can indicate how you live your life. There are two basic timeline perspectives – *through time* and *in time.*

The past, present and future memories of a through-time timeline may go from left to right or right to left or in any other direction; the distinction is that the entire timeline is in front of you and does not pass through you.

Characteristics of through-time people are as follows:

- Memories are usually dissociated – they can see themselves in the memory – and, as a result, they tend to show less emotion for sensitive or difficult memories.
- Because all time is in front of them, through-time people are aware of time – what they have done, what they are doing now, what they need to be doing – and may have less ability to enjoy the moment. They're punctual and expect punctuality in return. They are also aware of the duration of time and often see time and money as equivalent (the value of a service is equivalent to the amount of time spent).
- They look upon work as separate from play and will live a more organized, planned existence.
- They establish and are serious about deadlines.
- They are good at planning and enjoy using daytimers in which they can plan their day and week. They will also plan their vacations – and where and when they will do certain activities – in detail.

The in-time timeline is front to back – or back to front, yet in each case it runs through your body. The present is located in your body.

The following are characteristics of in-time people:

- They are fully associated when accessing memories. They will have a significant emotional response to sensitive or difficult memories.

- They can become caught up in the moment and may have trouble meeting their time commitments.
- They often do not differentiate between work and play.
- They tend not to plan and avoid setting deadlines.

If your timeline is some combination of through time and in time (for example, if part of your timeline is behind you and the timeline does not go through your body), you may exhibit a combination of the above characteristics. Time can be viewed as a meta program with the characteristics of through time and in time illustrating the two extremes.

Through their choice of words or body language, people often indicate their preference for through time or in time. For example, a person may say, "let's put that behind us" (as she gestures behind herself), or "let's set that aside" (as she points to the side), or "let's move forward on this" (as she points forward), or "let me get a larger perspective on what we have to do" (as she spreads her arms out in front).

Being through time or in time is neither good nor bad. However, there are situations in which one is preferred over the other. Through time is useful if you need to plan and get something done. In time is a better choice if you are spending a romantic evening with your spouse. Some people have the ability to switch between the two, depending on the circumstances. Other people have lived all of their lives from only one of these perspectives and have no understanding or compassion for someone who exhibits the other traits.

The structure of your timeline and what it may indicate

As we observed with the characteristics for through time and in time, there is an association between the structure of your timeline and how you live your life.

In their book, *Introducing NLP: Psychological Skills for Understanding and Influencing People* (pp. 136–7), Joseph O'Connor and John Seymour provide the following examples:

- If your past is out in front of you, it will always be in view; thus, your past will be an important and influential part of your life.
- If your future timeline consists of big, bright pictures, you are future-oriented. That is, your future is attractive and draws you compellingly toward it.
- If your future timeline is too compressed, with not enough space between future pictures, you may feel pressed for time, as everything looks like it has to be done at once.

In their article, "A Brief History of NLP Timelines" (*VAK International NLP Newsletter* Vol. 10, No. 1. Winter 1991–92), Steve and Connirae Andreas note that if your future timeline is in your visual constructed quadrant (up and to the right for most people, see chapter 3.3 – Eye accessing cues), then you could easily construct alternative futures rich with possibility. However, a future timeline in the visual remembered quadrant would result in a relatively specific and fixed future, because you have to use remembered imagery to represent the future. They refer to a man with this latter type of timeline, who said, "This makes perfect sense: 'change history' was always really easy for me, but never made my future different because that was still fixed."

Other examples of your timeline influencing or being a metaphor for how you live are:

- A dark future timeline may indicate you have no plans for or apprehension about the future.
- If all of your past timeline is inside your body, this may indicate your desire to keep the past to yourself.
- A past timeline that is a series of spirals may indicate that you have repeated a number of patterns in the past.
- Negative past memories directly in front may block your future.

A person's description of his timeline can give you great insight into how he lives his life.

Working with timelines

You can work with timelines through "theater of the mind," using mental images, or you can physically create and walk the timeline.

Theater of the mind

In your mind, visualize your timeline and its structure and relationship to you. Does it present itself fully out in front of you? Perhaps a part goes through you, or you see a series of clouds. Now, begin to dissociate by imagining stepping out of your body and floating higher and higher above your timeline. If you have a preference for visual, see yourself floating higher. If your preference is auditory, you may imagine yourself as a musical note, floating higher and higher. If kinesthetic, feel yourself being lifted higher and higher as if in a hot air balloon or floating on a warm breeze. The purpose of floating above the timeline is to dissociate from your memories so that you'll have less or no emotional response. If you require additional safety or if your memories are particularly emotional, you can imagine floating on a piece of Plexiglas. This will allow you to see and hear what is going on, but will block the feelings (another form of dissociation). Some people find it easier to push their timeline to the side rather than float above it. You can choose to dissociate from the timeline in whatever approach feels best to you.

Physically walking the timeline

Lay out a representation of your timeline on the floor – you can see this as an imaginary line on the floor or actually mark it with tape. No matter what the structure of your timeline, see the representation as a continuum on the floor. To dissociate from your timeline, simply step off to the side. As before, you can use an imaginary piece of Plexiglas between you and the timeline for extra dissociation and safety.

Both of these approaches have advantages.

- Theater of the mind:
    - o In a classroom setting, it provides some privacy and eliminates the problem of other people walking across your timeline and interrupting your process.
    - o If you want to float far back into your past or far into your future, you are not restricted by walls or other physical obstructions.
    - o You can float back in time or forward into the future very quickly.

- Physically walking the timeline:
    - o As a coach, you can see where your client is in relation to the present or past memory and potentially provide more guidance.
    - o You may prefer the physical activity of walking beside the timeline rather than doing everything in your mind.

Changing a timeline

Given that the structure of your timeline is associated with how you live your life, the following exercise illustrates how to change your timeline from through time to in time, or vice versa. This is best done through the theater of the mind.

1. Make yourself comfortable and close your eyes.

2. Imagine floating out of your body and well above your timeline.

3. With your real or imaginary hands, reach out and make the required change.

4. Float back down inside your body with the new structure for your timeline.

5. Stay seated for a few minutes and do not operate any equipment or drive

a car for at least fifteen minutes. If switching between through time and in time is not part of your daily routine, you may find this change to be somewhat destabilizing, and you may need time to adjust.

You may also find that your timeline will not change as you would like, or that it springs back to its former structure. This may be due to a perceived lack of safety, a fear of the consequences of the new behavior, or some other fundamental issues that need to be addressed. Lack of safety or fear of consequences can be handled by getting more information or support or by giving your unconscious mind permission to revert back to your original timeline whenever you feel unsafe.

As you address issues in your life, you may also find that the structure of your timeline changes in some way. You may find that you are more "through time" or more "in time" or more balanced – able to switch between the two – and dark areas in your past or future may become brighter.

Emotions and energy

Emotional responses such as anger, sadness and guilt are often referred to as unwanted or negative emotions. However, they are simply emotions that occur naturally and are part of being human. The problem arises when they become excessive compared to the situation that caused them. For some people, the term *emotions*, by itself, has a negative connotation or is something to be ashamed of. This shouldn't be the case. We all experience what we call emotions because we have energy flowing through part or all of our bodies. Yet we love to label things, and often tend to mislabel them. How often have you experienced excitement or passion about something, mislabeled it as anxiety, and subsequently took on less than optimal behaviors?

To get past the negative connotations and potential mislabeling, it is preferable to refer to energy, rather than emotions, moving through your body. With energy, it is important that it flows through and dissipates in the body. Energy blockages can result in physical ailments.

An intervention using timeline

This intervention can be used to address limiting beliefs or decisions or excess energy due to anger, sadness, fear, guilt or shame – for example, some of us live our lives driven by excess anger energy or guilt energy. To undertake this intervention, it is not necessary for you to know the structure of your timeline; you need only to acknowledge that a timeline exists. In the past, when you did not fully address your anger, sadness or fears, this energy could not fully metabolize in your body. Consequently, it remained blocked as an energy marker or flag.

The purpose of the energy marker is to remind you that there are unresolved issues or that you have something to learn from the events that caused the energy block. Once you've acquired this knowledge, the energy marker is no longer required and the energy dissipates.

This intervention is described for the theater of the mind technique. It can easily be adjusted for walking the timeline.

1. Identify the issue – the limiting belief or decision or excess energy associated with an emotion – to be addressed.

2. Make yourself comfortable and close your eyes.

3. Float above your timeline.

4. Acknowledge that there is a root cause for this issue. Agree to trust your unconscious mind to identify the cause, and to now transport you quickly and safely back to the time the issue first occurred – the root cause.

5. From the safety of your position well above your timeline and directly above the root cause event, ask yourself what you can learn from that event and, in particular, what you can learn about yourself. When the answers come to you – in NLP, we refer to these answers as *learnings* – have your unconscious put them in a special place so they're available whenever you need them in the future.

6. Once your unconscious has stored and saved these learnings, it can let the energy go, as this marker is no longer required. When you address a limiting belief or decision, your unconscious can also let the belief or decision go and implement a new belief or decision based on the new learnings.

7. Float further back into the past, above your timeline and well before the root cause event, and notice that the energy associated with this memory has disappeared. If it hasn't, float back even further into the past – above the timeline – and well before this event or any root cause event ever occurred. Since you are now in a place prior to the event's occurrence, it means the event has not happened and there is no energy marker. Alternatively, remind yourself that blocked energy in the body leads to disease and it is better to have the learnings and to let the energy go.

8. When you have released the energy, float down into the root cause event and notice that the energy really has dissipated. Notice anything else that you need to learn.

9. Float back above your timeline and begin to return to the present.

10. Test and future pace. Remaining above the timeline, float out into the future and notice what it will be like to live your life with these new learnings (and new belief or decision, if appropriate).

11. Float back to the present and down into your body.

Sometimes, when the energy from an emotion is cleared, a different emotion appears. For example, anger may mask fear, hurt or sadness. Once you are aware of these new emotions, you can work on them with the above exercise.

You may pose the question: "If I clear an emotion using this technique, does this mean that I will never experience that emotion again?" Reassuringly, the answer is no. It simply means you will display that emotion at a level that is appropriate for the situation. This exercise should be repeated on a regular basis. As we go through life we build up unresolved energy that needs to be dissipated before it builds to a critical mass.

The above is adapted from Timeline Therapy®, developed by Tad James and described in his book with Wyatt Woodsmall, *Timeline Therapy and the Basis of Personality* (Meta Publications, 1988).

6.3. DOCK OF THE BAY – ACCESSING ADDITIONAL RESOURCES

Every day we are presented with opportunities to make conscious or unconscious choices about how we respond to certain stimuli, behaviors or events. In NLP, we refer to these choices as *choice points*. Most of these choice points are minor – choosing between a glass of milk and a glass of water. However, some are significant, and they can set in motion a pattern or path for the way you live your life. How, for example, do you react to your spouse's tone of voice, if you perceive him or her to be angry? How do you behave when challenged during a job interview?

Recall the NLP presupposition that everyone does the best they can with the resources available to them. If, during a choice point, you recognize that you have more resources available to you, you have the potential of making better choices for yourself and your life.

Developed by NLP expert John Grinder, "dock of the bay" is an NLP technique designed to provide you with more resources for a specified choice point.

1. Identify a significant choice point, a time in your life when you acted in a less than resourceful way.

2. Imagine sitting on an imaginary dock on a serene lake, bay or body of water. Feel the warm sun on your body, a soft breeze caressing your face, or

any special sounds or smells. The idea is to be in as relaxed and resourceful a state as possible, as you sit on the dock.

3. Picture someone who looks and sounds like you on an island far in the distance; someone who is going through an identical choice point. Acknowledge that the person on the island could be making better choices.

4. What resources do you think the person on the island could use to improve his situation?

5. Recall a time when you had the resources the person on the island needs, or imagine someone who has these resources. You do not have to personally know this person. This person could be a character in a TV show, a colleague, or anyone who truly has the required resources.

6. Step off the dock. Step back into your own body or into the body of the person with the required resources. Assume the posture, feelings, voice tonality and any other important characteristics of that person to truly feel, absorb and take ownership of those resources.

7. Once you have truly assumed the required resources, return to the dock, but only as quickly as you can bring all of the resources back with you.

8. After you return to the dock with your new resources, notice that the person on the island has also acquired these resources.

9. Watch the person on the island rerun the choice point scenario from beginning to end.

10. How is the person on the island, who looks like you, doing? Could that person use more resources? If yes, repeat steps four through ten.

11. Once the person on the island is able to run the choice point scenario from beginning to end in a truly resourceful manner, invite the person on the island who looks like you to join you on the dock. Once the person is on the dock, wrap your arms around this person, hold the person close and absorb the feelings. Combine both of your resources together. As the integration is taking place, you may wish to tell the other person that you love and accept this person, and that this person is now safe.

12. Test and future pace.

6.4. SIX-STEP REFRAME –INCREASING UNCONSCIOUS CHOICE IN AN ECOLOGICAL WAY

The six-step reframe is used to increase a client's behavior options in situations where the client realizes his behavior is causing problems. Behavior is interpreted in a very wide sense, including allergies and physical symptoms. For example, allergies can be considered a behavior of the immune system. The six-step reframe was developed by John Grinder in the early 1980s as part of a series of patterns that form the foundation for NLP new code – a reformulation of basic NLP principles and processes. NLP new code was developed by John Grinder and Judith DeLozier in the late 1980s and described in their book *Turtles All the Way Down* (Grinder and Associates, 1987).

The basis of the six-step reframe is as follows:

- The assumption that the client has an internal "part" of him that is responsible for this behavior.
- The NLP presupposition: every behavior has a positive intention.
- Establishing a means of communication with the part. Direct communication with the part is established through a series of questions with yes/no answers. When answering the questions, your client uses only the unconscious response without attempting to produce a conscious answer. As long as there is an effective means of communication with the part, the details do not need to be conscious.
- Ensuring the part feels safe and no judgment is made about its choice of behavior. The part does not need to be removed, as it has a positive intention.
- Developing new behavioral choices that satisfy the same higher-level positive intention but do not have the problematic side effects or consequences.
- The internal part approving and implementing the alternatives.
- Pacing the current experience by acknowledging the part exists and that it does have a positive intention. Leading by providing more appropriate ecological choices to achieve the positive intention.

As is the case with many NLP techniques, it's not necessary for your client to reveal what the problematic behavior is.

Six-step reframe – the process

The following steps are based upon text provided by my friends and colleagues Graham and Denise Wright:

1. Ask your client to focus on the behavior or symptom and to assign it a neutral name, for example, "exing." The name or label should be one that elicits a neutral response in your client. Nonsense words or mathematical symbols also work well.

   As a coach, the next step is to say to your client, "Make yourself comfortable. Place your complete attention on the behavior or symptom you wish to change and give it a neutral name" – assume they say "exing." Ask your client, "Is the part responsible for 'exing' willing to communicate via an unconscious signal?"

Your client uses an unconscious signal to answer yes or no. If a no response is obtained, there is a rapport or safety issue to be resolved. A yes response must be obtained before moving forward in all steps except step four.

The unconscious signal can be involuntary finger movements, a twitching of an eye, a specific feeling somewhere in your client's body, such as a gut feeling. It may be subtle and it should be something that the client is not controlling consciously. Other unconscious physiological responses such as muscle testing (from kinesiology) or dowsing can also be used to access the unconscious responses to the questions. To use the signal, your client simply observes the physiological response when asked a yes/no question. Your client does not need to consciously find an answer nor necessarily understand the question. As the coach, you must ask yes/no questions, as the signal is not set up for multiple choices.

2. Obtain permission to create three new behaviors that satisfy the positive intention. Here is dialogue you can use effectively:

Coach: "I would like to thank the part responsible for "exing" for its positive intention and ask that part if it is willing to get together with the creative part to create three new behaviors, for use in an "exing" situation, that get the same positive intention as "exing" *and* are acceptable to all parts of you. Is it willing to do that?"

Every behavior is presupposed to have a positive intention, which may not, and does not, need to be consciously known by your client or you. Three behaviors are used because one behavior is stuck, two are a dilemma, and three give choices. The tag question is needed to elicit the yes/no answer. Your client's conscious mind does not need to understand the questions.

Client uses unconscious signal to answer yes or no.

Coach: "I would like to ask the creative part if it is willing to get together with the part responsible for "exing" and create three new behaviors for use in an "exing" situation that are acceptable to all parts of you; is it willing to do that?"

Client uses unconscious signal to answer yes or no.

3. Create three new behaviors.

Coach: "I would like to ask the part responsible for "exing" and the creative part to get together and create three new behaviors in an "exing" situation that get the same positive intention as "exing" *and* that are acceptable to all parts of you and let us know when they have done that; are they willing to do that *now*?"

Client uses unconscious response to answer yes or no.

Coach: Wait and watch. When it appears the action is complete, check it out. "Have these three new behaviors been created?" It is not necessary – and may not be useful – for your client to know consciously what any of these new behaviors are.

Client uses unconscious response to answer yes or no.

4.   Ecology check. Determine if any other parts object to the new choices.

Coach: "Are there any parts that object to any of these new behaviors?"

This is extremely important. If a yes answer is obtained, then go back to step three and include the objecting part in the new behavior creation process. If there are safety issues, include the part responsible for safety.

Client uses unconscious response to answer yes or no.

5.   Implementing the new choices.

Coach: "Is the part that chooses behaviors willing to choose one or more of these new behaviors in an "exing" situation?"

The new behaviors will be offered as a choice to be made at the time of a future "exing" situation (i.e., they are not imposed). The unconscious mind will make the best choice available to it at the time. The original behavior is not deleted, as there may be some circumstances where this is still the best choice.

Client uses unconscious response to answer yes or no.

6.   Finishing up.

Coach: "I would like to thank all the parts that participated for their good work."

NLP is conducted in an atmosphere of politeness and respect, even for parts that have a seemingly negative behavioral result.

Identifying a signal for yes and no

Signal for yes: Think of a time when you really wanted something and you were fully congruent in obtaining it. Associate into that event and notice what it feels like to be fully congruent. Repeat this for several other occasions and notice what feelings were present in all situations. This becomes your signal for yes.

Signal for no: Think of a time when you had reservations about something, when something just didn't feel right. Associate into that event and notice what it feels like to be uncertain or hesitant. Repeat this for several other occasions and notice what feelings were present in all situations. This is your signal for no or incongruence. Being consciously aware of your signal for no can save you from making inappropriate decisions as you go through your daily activities.

6.5. FORGIVENESS

At some point in our lives, all of us have been wronged by another person and felt hurt, angry or resentful. This is a natural reaction and part of being human. However, if we do not resolve or come to terms with these hurts, they drive our actions and create a negative way of life. By harboring past hurts, we have the potential to do far more harm to ourselves than anyone else can possibly do.

> "All illness is caused by not forgiving."
> – *Native American belief*

Forgiving others – or yourself – does not mean forgetting or condoning what happened, giving up the values that were violated or assuming you are at fault; nor does it mean condemning the other person or seeking justice or compensation. Forgiveness can be viewed as foregoing the resentment or revenge when the wrongdoer's action deserves it and giving the gifts of mercy, generosity and love when the wrongdoer does not seem to deserve them. To release the shackles of the past, we must be willing to forgive.

Forgiveness is about creating a state "for giving" – both to self and others – and excusing a mistake or an offense and letting go of the associated hurt, anger or resentment. Because forgiveness has the greatest benefit to the person doing the forgiving, it is one of the greatest gifts that you can give to yourself.

Forgiving allows us to get on with our lives and to open up our minds and hearts to new ways of seeing others, the world and ourselves. It releases energy that can be used for other, more productive thoughts and actions.

The forgiveness pattern

The foundation for the following pattern is the work of Connirae and Steve Andreas. This version comprises many more steps than their original work. Some of the steps may be omitted, depending on how tightly your client is clinging to a non-forgiving state.

The purpose of this pattern is to bring peace and resolution to the person who feels hurt, angry or resentful. Forgiving will make it much easier to take effective action as well as upholding your values and standards in the future.

1. Identify a situation in which you still harbor anger, animosity or resentment toward someone or where someone has caused you pain. Ideally, this should be someone with whom you would like to reach a feeling of forgiveness and resolution.

   You must be willing to at least consider forgiving the other person. Steps two and three are intended to open up the possibility of forgiving.

2. Review the following presuppositions and keep them in mind as you go through this exercise:

   • Every behavior has a positive intention.

   • Everyone is doing the best they can with the resources available to them.

   • The system or person with the most flexibility of behavior will have the most influence on the system.

3. Use perceptual positions to gain different perspectives.

   • A representative situation in the past: Consider the particular situation or, if it's a series of situations, select a representative situation and review it from all four perceptual positions. Remember to break state between each position. You may wish to visit some positions more than once. Some questions to consider are:

     o First position: Have I accidentally misinterpreted the actions of the other person?

     o Second position: What might be the positive intentions behind the other person's actions? Do I now have a better understanding of the other person's limitations? What might have been her original intentions?

     o Third position: How would an independent third party view the other person's actions? What advice would she give to me to avoid such a situation in the future?

     o Fourth position: Does this new perspective give me some insight into how the larger system assisted in creating this situation? Are there other actions that I might have taken to avoid this problematic situation?

   • Current impact: Approach the current situation from all four perceptual positions. Some questions to consider are:

     o First position: What is the positive intention behind not forgiving the other person? Could I achieve this positive intention another way? What am I gaining or achieving as a result of not forgiving? How could things be different if I were to forgive?

- o Second position: What are the results of my actions on the other person?

- o Third position: How would an independent third party view my actions?

- o Fourth position: What are the results of my actions on the larger system – my employer, for example – and what are the potential consequences for me?

- • Future impact: Consider a time, one, five or ten years in the future from all four perceptual positions. Some questions to consider are:

- o First position: What have I achieved as a result of not forgiving? How might things have been different if I had forgiven?

- o Second position: What have the effects of my actions and unforgiveness been (if any) on the other person?

- o Third position: How would an independent third party view my actions and the resulting consequences?

- o Fourth position: What have been the results of my actions on the larger system, and what have been the consequences for me?

4. Use submodalities to engender forgiveness.

   a. Think of someone you have already forgiven.

   b. Elicit the submodalities of this memory and the submodalities of the situation in step one. Identify those submodalities that are different between the two situations.

   c. Referring back to the situation in step one, change the submodalities, one at a time, to the submodalities elicited for step four (a).

5. Access resources and forgiving.

   a. Focus your thoughts on a representative situation in the past. Use your imagination to explore what internal resources would benefit the other person in this situation. Now think of a time when you've had these resources yourself.

   b. Mark out a space on the floor called "resources." Using removable tape is an effective method. Then step into that resource space and relive the time when you were fully able to access this resource.

c. While you are standing in your resource space, imagine sending these resources to the person with whom you've had the conflict. Imagine watching him or her behave differently than in the original situation, because of these new resources.

d. Still standing in your resource space, revisit this situation from the four perceptual positions, with the other person acting in the new and resourceful way.

e. Step out of the resource space and create a new, forgiveness space on the floor. Find a time when you fully forgave someone. Relive that time. At the peak of your forgiveness, step into your forgiveness space and create a strong association – anchor – between the feeling and the forgiveness space.

f. Standing in the forgiveness space, forgive the other person completely, wishing them all the happiness and fulfillment they desire from life. Reach out and imagine touching that person's shoulders. Look him or her in the eyes and say, "I forgive you."

6. Step into the resource space and review from the four perceptual positions what might happen the next time you encounter the person – or think of them if the person is deceased.

7. Address possible resistance.

Does any part of you object to forgiving this other person? If yes:

- Reframe any objections, potentially using the information gained from step three, until the change is acceptable.

- If the concern is losing the positive benefits associated with not forgiving (e.g., safety), find other, more favorable ways to maintain this benefit.

- Remember that forgiving does not condone the other person's behavior, nor does it mean you have to change your values.

- Repeat steps four or five, if necessary.

8. Future pace and test, using the following methods:

a. Rehearse your new behaviors and decisions in future situations so that your actions occur naturally and instinctively.

b. Think of the person toward whom you used to feel resentment/anger. Objectively assess how you feel about this person now.

c. Project yourself to a time in the future and assess the situation from the four perceptual positions.

6.6. WORKING WITH PARTS – RESOLVING CONFLICTS

Many of our outcomes for career, family, romance, health and purpose in life arc bascd on the requests, desires or expectations of others – parents, spouse, teachers, religious leaders, boss and society. Yet these are not our personal outcomes, and therefore do not provide the energy that propels us forward to truly achieve our highest potential. When we struggle with our outcomes, almost always there is some hidden inner conflict that needs resolution. Often we are less than fully alive because of these inner conflicts.

Sometimes you may have an internal conflict or incongruence about some aspect of yourself and feel as it you are of "two minds" on the issue. In NLP we call these parts, and each is capable of having different intentions and functioning independently of the other. You may experience a conflict between: your job and spending time with your family; your career and your health; being entrepreneurial and playing it safe; freedom and settling down with someone special.

A parts conflict is often revealed through the words you use. These can be phrases such as "on the one hand," "I feel torn about this," or "a part of me agrees with you." Your behaviors may suggest different attitudes, and those attitudes may vary in different contexts. You may have one set of behaviors at work and a different set at home. Here's an important question you may ask yourself: If your co-workers and family members happen to be gathered together at the same place and the same time, which set of behaviors would you display – who would you choose to be?

From the viewpoint of logical levels, parts – in conflict – may form at the following levels: 1) spiritual (your purpose in life), 2) identity (who you see yourself being), 3) beliefs/values (health or career), and 4) capabilities/strategies (skills or strategies to be a good parent or not, for example). The higher the logical level at which the parts form, the more pervasive the impact. Parts at the identity level will have their own supporting beliefs and values as well as different capabilities and strategies and may act as different entities altogether.

The notion of "parts" originated with the works of family therapist Virginia Satir and Gestalt therapy founder Fritz Perls. Refer to Virginia Satir, *Peoplemaking* (Science and Behavior Books, Inc., 1972). Some NLP practitioners argue that individuals should not have any parts. My personal view is that people can have parts, as long as the parts are working in a holistic sense. For example, it is nice to know that I have a creative part, a compassionate part, a part that is working on my safety or one that is giving me new challenges. These parts express different aspects of my nature that I'm able to access when I need specific assistance. However, a problem may arise when two or more parts are in conflict and do not co-operate with each other.

The *visual squash* is a NLP technique that was created by Richard Bandler and John Grinder in the 1970s (*The Structure of Magic*, Volume II, Science and Behavior Books, 1976). Its purpose is to integrate conflicting parts. Since then, it has developed and evolved in a number of ways to include exploring the positive intention of each part by chunking up, negotiation between the parts, as well as reframing. This revised technique, described below, is often referred to as *parts integration*.

1. Identify the conflict or incongruence and the parts involved. Make sure you identify the parts clearly and understand the nature of the conflict or incongruence.

    Some NLP practitioners refer to one part in a positive way and the other part in a negative way – the desired state or behavior versus the unwanted state or behavior. Recognize that this may be a judgment call. What must be understood is that each part has a positive intention. Using judgments without examination of the reasons behind them only creates more conflict between the parts.

2. Invite one of the parts to come out on one of your client's hands. Elicit a visual, auditory and kinesthetic description of the part.

    Sometimes a part is reluctant to come out – most often for safety reasons. If this is the case, you may decide to give it permission to return inside whenever it feels unsafe, you may say you are there to ensure both parts are safe and to permit each part to express itself freely, or you may surround a part with imaginary Plexiglas.

    As your client describes the visual, auditory and kinesthetic description of the part, pay attention to the metaphor. This may give you important information for later steps.

3. Invite the other part to come out on the other hand. Elicit a visual, auditory and kinesthetic description of this part.

4. Separate intention from behavior. Start with one of the parts. Ask the part, "What is your intention or purpose?" Continue asking, "What is your intention?" or "For what purpose?" as you have the part chunk up to a higher level of thought or abstraction.

5. Ask the other part "What is your intention or purpose?" Continue asking, "What is the intention?" or "For what purpose?" as you have the part chunk up to a higher level of thought or abstraction.

    If you find that the parts do not have the same overall intention, you may have to repeat steps four and five. Have each part recognize and acknowledge the positive intent of the other. At some point, the parts will realize – possibly with your help – that they have the same overall intention. That intention may be continued well-being or be as high as existence. At this time, you may notice that your client's hands begin to come together. You can assist in furthering this process by 1) using embedded commands, and 2) leading your client with visual techniques, such as by bringing your own hands together slowly.

6. If your client's hands have not fully come together, you may ask your client to turn her hands so that both parts can see each other. Ask each part, "What resources or attributes does the other part have that it would like to have access to?"

7. As her hands come together, you may:

    a. Invite the parts to notice that they were once part of a larger whole.

    b. Ask if there are any other parts that would benefit from being part of this integration. Request that they also engage in this process.

8. Once her hands have come together, invite your client to identify an area, of her body, where this reintegrated energy belongs. Have her bring it inside.

9. Test and future pace.

If your client's hands do not automatically come together, use these suggestions:

*   Reframe or make use of each part's metaphor to encourage them to come together. I recall two men working on this exercise in one of our practitioner trainings. The client had both parts out on his hands, both parts had the same intention, and each had resources that the other could use; still, his hands were not coming together. One of the client's parts was a book. Not knowing what else to do, the practitioner asked the client if he had ever opened the book. The answer was no. The practitioner asked the client to open the book and see what was inside. When the client did so, his physiology changed and his hands immediately came together.

*   Ask your client what would be required for the parts to come together easily and effortlessly. Follow your client's lead.

6.7. V-K DISSOCIATION – DEALING WITH DISTRESSING OR TRAUMATIC EVENTS

Sometimes we need some space or distance from our feelings. This is particularly true if there is a very strong overlap or synesthesia between our visual and kinesthetic senses that leads us to an overwhelming debilitating state.

The V-K dissociation technique was one of the first techniques developed by Richard Bandler and John Grinder from their modeling of Milton Erickson and Fritz Perls. The purpose of the V-K dissociation technique is to separate the client's visual memories from his feelings. You will see parts of this technique incorporated in other techniques, wherever the client needs this separation.

The process

1. Have your client imagine he is sitting in a movie theater. A comfortable distance in front of him is a blank movie screen on which he can project various events. Ask your client to be relaxed, with his shoulders back, and looking up at the movie screen (about a twenty-degree angle).

   Notice how a separation – dissociation – is being set up between the event (and the feelings that go with it) and your client and what he sees. This is the first of several separations.

   Your client has a relaxed, comfortable physiology and his eyes are up in visual, not down in kinesthetic.

2. Have your client imagine that he is floating out of his body to a place behind him – perhaps into the projection booth.

   If you have the space, it can be useful for your client actually to move to a location farther back so he can see himself looking at the movie screen.

   If your client needs additional dissociation or safety, you can have him imagine that he is floating in the air, watching himself in the projection booth as he watches himself in the movie theater looking at the movie screen. Or you can have him imagine that in the projection booth he is completely surrounded by Plexiglas that he can look through and feel perfectly safe.

3. With your client feeling very resourceful and safe in the projection booth, anchor this safe and resourceful state so you can assist him in returning to it in the event he gets into the feelings associated with what is happening. A touch – a kinesthetic anchor – works best.

4. Have your client project snapshots of the distressful or traumatic event on the movie screen. Make sure these are still pictures surrounded by a frame.

To enhance the dissociation from any negative feelings, your client can change the submodalities by moving the pictures farther away, reducing the size or brightness or making them black and white. Have him do whatever is necessary to separate from any unwanted feelings.

In this and the next step, use language to remind your client that he is safe in the projection booth watching a younger version of himself. For example, say to him, "From the safety of the projection booth, see yourself watching a younger you in that event, over there."

5. Have your client make the still pictures into a movie (keeping any of the submodality changes from the previous step), while watching from the safety of the projection booth. Ask him to identify something new or something not previously remembered from this perspective – positive intention(s) or secondary gain(s). Ask your client to identify other choices that could be made and resources that could be used.

6. If necessary, call a time-out while you assist your client in accessing and anchoring these additional resources.

7. Have your client take all these new resources, learnings and choices with him as he safely floats from the projection booth back into his body in the movie theater.

8. From the seat in the movie theater, have your client imagine transferring these new resources, learnings and choices to the person in the movie. Have your client run the movie with all of these new resources, learnings and choices available to the person in the movie and check the ecology of the new choices.

9. Have your client reassociate himself into the past event with all of the resources, learnings and choices.

10. Future pace these changes for situations in the future that in the past would have been a trigger for the unwanted feelings. Ensure his new choices and resourceful physiology appear.

Phobias

A phobia is an irrational or intense fear of something. Common phobias include: fear of heights, flying, enclosed places, open spaces, social situations, animals, the dark and public speaking. A phobia can result from a single-trial learning experience that results in a generalization about the world and incorporates the fight-flight response.

Key to addressing a phobia is to identify the trigger that starts the phobic response and to have some knowledge of the initiating circumstances. The NLP approach to phobias is based on interrupting the pattern or program. The V-K dissociation model can be used, and you will notice in the following steps a number of aspects taken from this model.

Fast phobia cure

1. Establish a kinesthetic resource anchor for your client based on times when she was resourceful and safe.

2. Have her identify the trigger or context for the phobic response.

3. Have your client imagine she is sitting in a movie theater. A comfortable distance in front of her is a blank movie screen on which she can project various events. Ask your client to be relaxed, with her shoulders back, and looking up at the movie screen (about a twenty-degree angle).

4. Have your client imagine that she is floating out of her body to a place behind her – perhaps into the projection booth.

    If you have the space, it can be useful for your client to actually move to a location farther back so she can see herself looking at the movie screen.

    If your client needs additional dissociation or safety, you can have her imagine that she is floating in the air, watching herself in the projection booth as she watches herself in the movie theater looking at the movie screen. Alternatively, you can have her imagine that in the projection booth she is completely surrounded by Plexiglas that she can look through and feel perfectly safe.

5. From the projection booth, have your client imagine she can see a movie, projected on the movie screen, of the very first event that set-up the phobia (get the earliest possible memory, if she cannot remember the first event).

    To enhance the dissociation, your client can change the submodalities by moving the pictures farther away, reducing the size or brightness, or making them black and white. Whatever is necessary to separate from any unwanted feelings.

    In this and the next step, use language to remind your client that she is safe in the projection booth watching a younger version of herself. For example, say to your client, "From the safety of the projection booth, see yourself watching a younger you in that event, over there."

6. Have your client find times before and after the event when she was totally safe. Make sure your client can see the whole movie, beginning from the initial point of safety, through the frightening event, to the point of safety after the event.

7. Starting with the point of safety after the event, have your client run the movie backward. See all the events in reverse. Do this several times very quickly and break state between each time you repeat it.

8. Have your client explore the positive intention(s) or purpose of the fear. Ask your client to identify other choices that could be made and resources that could be used.

9. If necessary, call a time-out while you assist your client in accessing and anchoring these additional resources.

10. Have your client edit the movie by introducing the new resources, learnings and choices, and have her notice the positive effects these would have on that past event.

11. Have your client take all these new resources, learnings and choices with her as she safely floats from the projection booth back into her body in the movie theater.

12. From the seat in the movie theater, have your client imagine transferring these new resources, learnings and choices to the person in the movie. Have your client run the movie with all of these new resources, learnings and choices available to the person in the movie. Check the ecology of the new choices.

13. Have your client reassociate herself into the past event with all of the resources, learnings and choices, and have her notice what it is like.

14. Future pace these changes for situations in the future that in the past would have been a trigger for the unwanted feelings. Ensure her new choices and resourceful physiology appear.

After this procedure, it is possible your client will still have some anxiety, particularly if the original event involved actual danger. This is all right, as it is useful to be cautious with regard to potentially dangerous situations. The key is that the debilitating fear and irrational behavior are gone.

7.

Achieving What You Want in Life

IN NLP, WE PREFER TO FOCUS on outcomes rather than goals. The Merriam-Webster Online Dictionary defines a goal as "an end toward which effort is directed," while an outcome is defined as "something that follows as a result or consequence." Most people have great difficulty setting and achieving goals. However, we always achieve an outcome and if it is not what we want, we can view this as feedback and make appropriate changes to obtain a more acceptable outcome next time.

Have a clearly stated, meaningful outcome for everything you do – meeting with your boss, writing a report, dieting, exercising. How often have you not had a clearly stated outcome and, as a result, were co-opted to help someone achieve theirs. And afterward, have you "beaten them up" (or perhaps beaten yourself up) for being successful at your expense? Setting an outcome is the first step in the five steps for success. Each day, set at least one clearly stated outcome that is in alignment with your overall outcome for your family, career or life.

> If you do not know where you are going,
> you may end up somewhere else.
>
> – *Yogi Berra*

7.1. SPECIFYING YOUR OUTCOMES

To be successful in life, you need to know what you want, express it clearly and succinctly and have a passion for achieving it. To assist you in specifying your outcomes, we use outcome MASTERY and the NLP well-formed conditions. There is some overlap between the two, and sometimes it is useful to address a similar question from a different perspective.

	Outcome MASTERY
M	**Measurable** – How will you know if you are making progress and what must happen for you to know you have achieved your desired outcome? **Meaningful** – Is your outcome important for you?
A	**Achievable** – Do you believe your outcome is achievable? This is what you believe, not what others believe. **All areas of your life** – Are you fully congruent for achieving this outcome or are there conflicts (internal or external) that you need to resolve? **As if now** – From this moment on, live as if you already have achieved your outcome. Remember the young man in the financial institution? (Section 2.4)
S	**Specific and Simple** – Your outcome should describe clearly what you wish to achieve and should be expressed in very simple language and sentence structure. In this way, there is no confusion on the part of your unconscious mind as to what needs to be done. The outcome, "I want more money" is simple, yet not specific. It does not specify when I would like this to happen or how much more money. If someone were to give me one penny, my outcome would be achieved. If your outcome is an emotional state, such as being happy or confident, you can achieve this now by changing your internal representations. Instead, you may wish to phrase your outcome as having control over your emotional states.
T	**Timed** – You must specify an exact time. Saying tomorrow or next month is not adequate – tomorrow will always be tomorrow. **Toward what you want** – What you focus on is what you get. If your outcome is, "I don't want to fail," your focus will be on failing. You will then notice all the signs of potential failure rather than the signs of success. Focusing on what you don't want implies that anything else is acceptable and the outcome you achieve may be worse than what you have now.

E	**Ecological** – Is your outcome in alignment with your values? What is the potential impact now and in the future on those systems of which you are a member (family, work) and your health and well-being (internal systems)?
R	**Realistic** – Is your outcome realistic according to you? It does not have to be realistic in the minds of others. **Responsible** – Be at cause; assume responsibility for your actions and the consequences of achieving your outcome.
Y	**Yearning** – Without a real yearning or passion for achieving your outcome, it is only a series of words. Your passion will drive your activities and success. It will dominate your conversations, thinking, actions and your very being. To be passionate about an outcome, it must be in alignment with your values. You will fail to achieve an outcome if it is too bland, too lifeless or is one that someone else has imposed on you. In life, it is not necessarily the smartest or most gifted that succeed, but those with desire.

Well-formed conditions

To construct a well-formed outcome:

- Specify the outcome and context. What specifically do you want? Where, when and with whom will you achieve your outcome?

- State your outcome in positive terms.

- Specify your present situation. Where are you now in relation to achieving this outcome?

- Specify the evidence procedure. How will you know you have achieved your outcome? What will you see, hear and feel when you have achieved it?

- Make the outcome compelling. Determine what has stopped you from achieving this outcome in the past. Is it too big or small for you?

  o Chunk down if the size of the outcome overwhelms you. If your outcome is too big, you may not know where to start, or you may nibble at the edges without making any real progress.

  o Chunk up if you find the chunks too boring or easy to accomplish. Ask yourself, "What will this outcome obtain for me or allow me to do?" Obstacles will disappear if you link your outcome to something that is important to you.

- Determine if the outcome is within your control. Is it something you can initiate and maintain yourself? The more your outcome depends on other people, the less control you have, and your chances of success diminish accordingly.

A well-formed outcome is not about other people changing. It is about changes in you that may result in a change in their behavior. An outcome such as, "my wife will spend more time with me," is one that is not within your control. Consider instead, "I am, in all of my actions, beliefs and values, the type of person she would like to spend time with." Make sure this is ecological, otherwise you may feel you have given up your own needs to satisfy hers, and she may still not spend time with you.

- Determine the resources you need, such as skills, time, financing or education. Do you have the resources to initiate and maintain the outcome? If not, how will you get them?

Ask for assistance and advice. Many people never achieve their dreams simply because they never ask for help. Be persistent in asking and finding those who can help you. After all, how serious are you about achieving this outcome? Colonel Sanders of Kentucky Fried Chicken asked *1,009* times before someone purchased his chicken recipe. At each rejection, he used his sensory acuity to learn from the experience and to change his approach accordingly. He persisted until he was successful. Why? Because he believed in what he was doing, was fully committed and was passionate about his outcome.

- Check ecology. Are there any undesirable by-products? Have you preserved the positive by-products of the current situation?

7.2. IDENTIFYING AND ACHIEVING OUTCOMES

The following process enables you to go beyond setting an outcome to actually "program" your mind to achieve your desired outcome. This is a detailed approach that you may wish to modify to suit your needs.

1. Decide on your outcomes.

   a. Prepare a list of all of your dreams. Explore different contexts such as family and friends, recreation, financial, work or profession, health and spirituality. Answering the following questions may help you prepare this list:

o What do you wish to achieve in six months, one, five, ten or twenty years?

o As you sit in your rocking chair looking back on your life, what will you say was your greatest achievement?

o How do you wish to be viewed by family, friends and colleagues?

o What is most important to you?

o What brings you joy?

b. Categorize your dreams according to family and friends, recreation, financial, work or profession, health and spirituality. Also identify when you would like to accomplish your dreams – six months, one year, two, five, ten or twenty years. You should have dreams that are short- and long-term and that cover most of the categories.

c. Identify five major outcomes that you would like to achieve. Take the results of 1(b) and group similar dreams together. Notice that some are stepping stones to a much larger dream. Address any perceived conflicts.

d. For each of these five outcomes, write at least one paragraph stating why achieving this outcome is important to you – include as many benefits as you can possibly think of. If, after writing the paragraphs, you find that there is not a great deal of hunger, drive or passion for one or more of the outcomes, first make sure it's your outcome and not an outcome that others expect of you. Second, chunk down on those outcomes that seem too large or overwhelming or chunk up on those outcomes that seem boring or trivial.

2. Write down your outcomes.

Some people avoid writing their outcomes or setting long-term outcomes because they fear being locked into a course of action that will reduce their flexibility. It's important to remember that outcomes can be rewritten and this process revisited whenever new information comes to light or a change in direction is required.

Writing down your outcomes can be the difference between success and failure:

A study conducted at Yale University found that only three percent of its 1953 graduating class had clear written outcomes and plans to achieve them. The same class was surveyed twenty years later and it was discovered that the same three percent had greater financial net worth than the remaining ninety-seven percent combined! In addition, the three percent group had better health, relationships and social skills.

Writing your outcomes down is powerful. Reviewing what you have written, editing and rephrasing it to make it more concise and adding motivating words and action verbs allows you to clearly see your outcome, get a grasp of it and ensure that it sounds right and is ecological. It also gives you the tastes and smells of accomplishment. This will make your outcome more real and more achievable.

    a.   Ensure your description of your outcomes follows the MASTERY format.

    b.   Use the logical levels to add additional clarity to your outcome:

       o   Spirituality: What is your connection to the larger system of family, work and community? What is your purpose?

       o   Identity: Who will you be? What is your mission?

       o   Beliefs and values: What beliefs will you have about yourself and others? What will you value?

       o   Capabilities/strategies: What skills and resources will you have and what strategies will you have used to achieve your outcome?

       o   Behavior: What will other people observe about you when you achieve your outcome?

       o   Environment: Where, when and with whom will you be when you achieve your outcome?

    c.   Make sure your outcomes satisfy the well-formed conditions.

    d.   Make an exciting, clearly stated action plan for each outcome. Prioritize and sequence activities with clearly specified, reasonable dates. You may wish to start where you are today and plan forward. Or, you can begin by assuming you have achieved outcome and ask yourself what the step was just before achieving your outcome, and the step before that – i.e., work backward.

3.   Use the Disney creativity strategy.

The Disney creativity strategy can be used to gain more clarity and increased passion for your outcomes. Combine this strategy with mastermind groups or with the theater of the mind to gain even more clarity:

    a.   Mastermind groups.

Mastermind groups consist of people with different interests and skills. These groups have the potential to help you see things differently, provide support and encouragement, and identify and open doors of which you may not have been otherwise aware. Mastermind groups share the basic philosophy that more can be accomplished in less time by working together. A mastermind group can be held in person or on a telephone bridge conference line.

b. Theater of the mind.

o   Identify three people who have the knowledge or expertise to advise you on your outcome. These people can be real or fictitious, alive or dead. You can change these people any time you need different advice.

o   Make yourself comfortable, close your eyes and journey inside to a special place called "sanctuary." You can go to sanctuary any time you need a time-out, a place of safety to contemplate your course of action, or to get advice from your advisors.

o   You are in charge of designing the sanctuary. It can be anywhere you choose – next to a body of water, inside your home or at a special vacation spot that helps you to relax. Make sure your sanctuary has the following: 1) a place to relax, 2) a place to work, 3) a source of information (library or computer), 4) a place to shred and dispose of unwanted baggage or limiting beliefs, 5) a screen on which you can play various scenarios to get an understanding of the results of possible courses of action, and 6) an entrance and exit for your advisors. Include anything else that you feel you may need.

o   Invite your advisors into the sanctuary. Explain to them your desired outcome, and ask them for their advice and assistance as you go through the different steps of the Disney creativity strategy.

o   Remember, you are in charge. You should fully consider any and all advice received from your advisors, and you are the one who will make the final decision.

o   After receiving all the advice you need and deciding on a course of action, thank your advisors for coming and close down sanctuary until your next visit.

o   You can go to your sanctuary whenever you desire. It can be a long visit when you just need time to relax or a short visit to quickly confirm a course of action.

4. Place your outcome into your future.

   a. Be sure your outcome is stated using the MASTERY outline.

   b. Identify the last step – what is the last thing that has to happen so you know you have achieved your outcome?

   c. Make an internal representation of the last step: a visual, auditory, kinesthetic – and, if appropriate, olfactory and gustatory – representation. Be fully associated by looking through your own eyes.

   d. Adjust the submodalities to enhance the positive feelings – make the final step as real as possible.

   e. Once the submodalities have been adjusted, view the internal representation from a dissociated perspective – you are now able to see yourself in the internal representation. A dissociated perspective indicates to your unconscious mind that the outcome has not yet been achieved and hence draws you to it, that is, it maintains the motivation. An associated outcome will not be as motivating because it gives you the feeling that you have already achieved your outcome.

   f. Take the internal representation in your real – or imaginary – hands and begin to float out of your body and well above your timeline.

   g. Energize the internal representation with four deep breaths – breathe in through your nose, out through your mouth, and as you exhale, imagine all of the energy from your breath flowing even more life into the internal representation.

   h. Float out into the future above your timeline, until you are over that future time when this event will occur.

   i. Insert the internal representation into your timeline by letting it go and seeing it gently floating down and becoming part of your future timeline.

   j. Once the internal representation becomes part of your future timeline, notice that events realign themselves between the present and this future time to support the achievement of your outcome. Also notice this realignment extends far out into the future to provide ensuing benefits.

   k. Float back to the present, above your timeline, and then down to your body. Fully immerse yourself in enjoying the benefits of achieving your outcome. Your unconscious mind does not differentiate between what is imagined and what is real.

5. Take action. Persist or your dreams will evaporate into thin air. Those who take immediate action are much more likely to be successful.

    a. Once a day for the first week, briefly repeat the above steps (particularly step four). If you have new information or your outcome has changed, you can easily make changes. Then repeat each week until you have achieved your outcome.

    b. Each evening, assess your progress (remember, there is no failure, only feedback) and identify at least three activities you will undertake the following day that will move you closer to achieving your outcome. Achieving your outcomes requires that you keep at it each day with relentless determination.

Tom Watson, Sr., the first president of IBM, crediting the rapid success of IBM, says this: "We visualized what we wanted our company to be when it was done and every day we evaluated our actions and whether we were closer to the goal because of them."

7.3. TEAM BUILDING

The above process can easily be modified to assist businesses or teams in identifying and achieving desired outcomes. It can be a great component for a team-building exercise. For example:

- The team can first identify team outcomes, then identify the contribution that each member of the team can make individually to support the team outcome.
- Instead of floating out into the future, each person can imagine they are in a time machine that will take them to different times. In this way, they can experience the results of their actions.

In the following chapter we will examine more closely how NLP can be used in a business context.

8.

Making a Difference in Business

Just as the ideas and concepts in this book can make a significant difference in your life, so too can they make a difference in business. A business environment is simply a collection of people. For this group to be successful, they need:

- A shared outcome.
- A healthy work environment. The group members need to feel safe and respected, be able to resolve conflicting beliefs and values, and respect other people's models of the world.
- Effective and respectful communication (within and outside the group).
- Sensory acuity to be aware of shifts within their work group or their external work environment.
- Congruence in their commitment to a common purpose.

All the material in this book can be used in a business context. Play with the NLP concepts, let your imagination be your guide, and you may just be surprised at how many different methods you discover.

8.1. FIVE ESSENTIAL ACTIVITIES

The following five activities are essential for any endeavor, be it in business or elsewhere:

- Feel good about yourself.

    Put yourself in an optimal mental and physical state. Address limiting beliefs and internal conflicts. Organize your thoughts and internal representations to bring all of your mental resources to the task at hand.

- Create well-formed outcomes.

A well-formed outcome helps you to:

o Distinguish between what you think you want and what you really want.

o Establish sensory-specific criteria so you know if you are making progress and when you have achieved your outcome.

o Outline the steps and resources required to achieve your outcome.

- Establish rapport.

Rapport creates trust and openness for others to clearly receive your message and for you to discover their needs and desires. This provides the greatest potential for dovetailing your needs with theirs and achieving a win-win result.

- Use your sensory acuity.

Recognize and appreciate that people do have different needs and wants and they may experience the world differently from the way you do. Use rapport, the meta model and sensory acuity to gain clarity on their issues and desires.

- Experience the event from different perspectives and make appropriate adjustments.

Use perceptual positions to assess your initiative before, during and after the activity – from your perspective, that of key decision makers and an independent observer. Assess the impact on the overall system. Adjust your outcome and planned approach as required.

8.2. MEETINGS, NEGOTIATIONS AND PRESENTATIONS

This chapter focuses on three main business activities: meetings, negotiations and presentations. This information is equally applicable in other areas of your life – how often do you meet with, negotiate or attempt to influence or present ideas to significant people in your life whom you encounter in other than a business context?

Meetings, negotiations and presentations have three major phases:

- Planning.
- Carrying out the actual meeting, negotiation or presentation.
- Wrapping up and the next steps.

Unfortunately, we often forget about the first and last phases and focus solely on the second with less than optimal results.

In reality, negotiations and presentations are meetings. Negotiations are meetings where there is potential for disagreement, while presentations can occur as part of a larger meeting or can be viewed as a meeting with only one item on the agenda.

The following steps provide a general approach to all three. Depending on the situation, some steps will be emphasized more than others. Specific details related to meetings, negotiations and presentations are presented later.

Planning

1. Determine your purpose and establish a well-formed outcome.

   Is your intention to inform, persuade, sell or move to action? What will be your evidence that you have achieved your outcome?

2. Determine who will be attending. What do you know about them? What can you find out in advance about their beliefs, values, meta programs, needs and pressures?

3. Identify potential areas of agreement.

4. Identify potential conflicts and possible resolutions.

5. Develop different options for achieving your outcome.

6. Generally, participants most accurately remember the first or last few minutes of a meeting, negotiation or presentation. Cover your key points during these time periods.

7. Take into account the preferences of those in attendance – their representational systems and meta programs. For example, include visuals for those who are highly visual. If your audience is mainly composed of entrepreneurs, remember from meta programs (chapter 3.5) to use toward, options, internal and proactive language and to talk to them about new ideas.

8. Prepare metaphors that will present your ideas in a different manner or a new light.

9. Choose a location that is appropriate for the task and does not have negative anchors. The boss's office can be a negative anchor for an employee. A better location for an informal discussion is a neutral area such as in the cafeteria over a coffee.

10. Rehearse the meeting, negotiation or presentation using the four perceptual positions. You should have an understanding of the thinking processes, motives, and emotions of the other parties involved. After your rehearsal, notice what you have learned and make adjustments accordingly.

11. Put yourself in an optimal state. Establish resource anchors and resolve any limiting beliefs or internal conflicts you may have.

Carrying out the meeting, negotiation or presentation

1. Establish rapport by greeting attendees as they enter.

2. Establish the purpose and get consensus from the group that there is a reason for continuing.

3. Use the relevancy check to keep the process on track.

   When a participant raises a point that you do not feel is relevant, ask, "How does (the point or issue raised) relate to the stated purpose?"

   If the participant can verify that it is relevant, the discussion continues. Otherwise, the issue is placed in a "parking lot" for discussion at the end of this particular activity or at some other time.

4. Dovetail participants' outcomes with yours and work toward an agreement on a common outcome.

   - Use your sensory acuity to identify incongruence in the other participants and to assess how your message is being received.
   - Maintain rapport by matching and mirroring body physiology, predicates, meta programs, voice tonality and speed and shared experiences.
   - Establish and use anchors to maintain your state.
   - Use the meta model to gain clarity on participants' comments or questions.
   - Probe for the purpose behind any disagreements.
   - Determine the positive intention behind any behaviors and actions and find other ways to satisfy this positive intention.
   - Reframe objections to provide a different perspective.
   - Chunk up to get agreement, and then chunk down only as fast as you can maintain agreement and finalize the details.
   - Explore differences to identify potential trade-offs.
   - Develop options.
   - Use perceptual positions to gain feedback on your approach, to gain an understanding of the other person's strategies and needs, to get an independent or system perspective on how the meeting, negotiation or presentation is going and to suggest other courses of action.
   - To identify hidden agendas, use a conditional close: "If I do X, will you then do Y?"
   - Use double binds to move to resolution. "Would you like to finalize this now or tomorrow morning?"

Wrapping up and next steps

1. Summarize outcome(s) achieved, including time frames and responsibilities.

2. Test and future pace the agreement and observe congruence.

3. Identify the next steps.

4. Determine how you might improve, first through feedback from others on your team, then by replaying the process through the four perceptual positions.

8.3. MEETINGS

> Meetings are where minutes are kept and hours are wasted.
>
> *– Unknown*

Far too often this observation is true. Meetings are called with no explicit outcome other than, "We need to have a meeting." There are no outcomes set. The meeting is held and two hours later, as people are leaving, you hear, "What was the purpose of that meeting?" or "Who is following up on that item?" or "I don't understand what is expected of me." Without any other stated outcomes, you may congratulate yourself, since you did achieve your outcome – you held a meeting. In addition to the general structure above, here are some additional thoughts about meetings.

Planning

1. Have few regularly scheduled meetings. Many issues can be handled by e-mail or phone.

2. Identify the purpose of the meeting. Some meetings or agenda items are solely to convey information, others are for discussion and yet others simply to make a decision. This should be clearly stated and conveyed beforehand to those attending.

3. Determine the membership and agenda and distribute the agenda in advance.

   If you expect people to lead the discussion on an agenda item and respond to specific questions, inform them in advance so they can be prepared to carry out their duties and support you.

4. Choose a meeting place that is appropriate for the task. For example, a more formal business meeting might be held in the boardroom or an informal staff meeting could be held in the staff cafeteria or picnic area.

5. If you are not chairing the meeting, you have a role to play in supporting the chairperson. If she has not assigned a specific role for you, you should review the steps listed here in order to support her to the best of your ability.

Carrying out the meeting

1. Make a sensory check as participants enter. Are they alert, ready for the meeting? If not, determine why not. For example, one of your participants may have to make a call home and feels that he cannot do so because you expect him at the meeting. Where do you think his attention will be?

2. Dovetail participants' needs and expectations with your own and work toward achieving your outcome.

    - Ask for help in developing options and identifying preferences among several options.
    - If there is a stalemate, ask, "What would have to happen in order to achieve X?"
    - Give strongly Away From people a role to play. Away From people are looking for things that can go wrong. This can take the energy out of a discussion on positive possibilities or an effort to set an outcome for the team. Ask these people to wait until some ideas and concepts have been developed, at which time you will ask them to provide a critical assessment.
    - Summarize each major decision with time frames and responsibilities. It is often best to have the person responsible for carrying out the decision to summarize. In this way, you can verify that she fully understands what needs to be achieved.

Wrapping up and next steps

1. Summarize outcome(s) achieved, including time frames and responsibilities.

8.4. NEGOTIATIONS

We regularly negotiate or desire others to buy into our ideas or suggestions. And often we are not successful because we have not planned our approach nor taken into consideration the other person's needs and concerns. We negotiate with members of our family, acquaintances, colleagues, supervisors and store clerks, to name a few. The most rewarding and satisfying negotiation is win-win, which leaves both participants with a willingness to enter into future transactions with the other party. Negotiation is the process of getting what you want from others by giving them what they want. The clearer you are about what you want and what you are prepared to give up, the more you protect yourself and generate trust.

Often negotiations take place over perceived scarce resources – e.g., this is the only house that meets my needs. Always have an alternative available so that you don't become locked into this perception and give away more than you want.

Planning

1. Develop different options for achieving your outcome. Avoid a fixed position and define upper and lower limits of what you are willing to accept or give.

2. Undertake research. With whom are you negotiating? What do you know about them? What can you discover about their beliefs and values, strategies, needs and pressures?

3. Determine your best alternative to an agreement (BATNA). Sometimes it is not possible to reach an agreement and you may choose to walk away. You need a BATNA, otherwise you will become stuck in the negotiation and eventually cave in to the other person's demands. Invariably, you will regret your actions later.

Carrying out the negotiation

1. Establish the negotiation as a joint effort to reach a mutually acceptable agreement.

2. Ensure the other person is serious about negotiating. If an issue keeps getting in the way, ask him, "What would happen if I were able to resolve this concern?"

3. Determine the other person's outcome. How will they know when they have achieved it (evidence)?

4. Identify areas of agreement and ensure a common understanding.

5. Dovetail outcomes and work toward an agreement on a common outcome.

   - If the negotiation is going off track, using rapport, ask, "How is this relevant to the agreed purpose of the negotiation?"
   - Ask for help in developing options and identifying preferences among several options.
   - Chunk up to get agreement, and then chunk down only as fast as you can maintain agreement and finalize the details.
   - Remember your best alternative to an agreement and be prepared to act upon it.

- Get agreement on the best option and move to close.
- **Important:** Don't negotiate with your team in front of the other team. If an option is raised and you need more time or information, ask for a break or schedule another session.

Wrapping up and next steps

1. Assess the impact – the ecology – of the agreement on yourself and others.

2. Summarize the agreement and identify the next steps.

3. Write down and have the agreement signed.

8.5. PRESENTATIONS

A presentation is a powerful way to communicate your message to a group. It's an opportunity to speak to a group where you decide on the message and lead the discussion.

Planning

1. Identify your purpose. Is your intention to inform, persuade, sell or move to action? What will be your evidence that you have achieved your outcome?

2. Decide how you will handle questions – during the presentation, afterward or not at all.

3. Prepare your presentation, taking into account different learning styles and preferred representational systems.

   The 4MAT System developed by Bernice McCarthy (*The 4MAT System: Teaching to Learning Styles with Right/Left Mode Techniques*, Illinois, USA: Excel Incorporated, 1981) identifies four learning styles:

   - Why? These people learn best by discussing the reasons why. Until they get this answered, they will not pay attention to your presentation. About thirty-five percent of the U.S. population have this learning style.
   - What? These people learn best when you give them information – facts and figures – either orally or on a handout. About twenty-two percent have this learning style.
   - How? These people learn best by doing and being coached. They want a hands-on approach. This is the learning style for about eighteen percent of the U.S. population.
   - What if? These people learn best through self-discovery. They explore the question, "I wonder what would happen if I did it a different way?" About twenty-five percent have this learning style.

Generally, the best approach is to structure your presentation to answer the four questions in the order presented. Some overlap and intermixing is fine. You may wish to start with a mini "What?" – tell your audience what you plan to tell them.

4. Check out the location for the presentation beforehand. Be sure it is suitable for the type of presentation you are giving and there is enough space for your audience, your equipment and you.

Carrying out the presentation

1. During the presentation, establish rapport by matching predicates, meta programs, voice tonality and speed and shared experiences.

Begin your presentation by speaking slowly in a low-pitched voice, but within your natural range, using kinesthetic predicates. After a few minutes, speed up, raise the pitch of your voice and introduce auditory predicates. Finally, speak faster – again within your natural range – while increasing your pitch and use of visual predicates. Many charismatic speakers start their presentations in this way. That is, they begin by first speaking to the kinesthetics, who take a little longer getting in touch with what you have to say, then to the auditories, and finally the visuals, who can quickly form a picture of what you are saying. Be sure to include some facts and figures that are logically connected and make sense for those with an auditory digital preference. Vary this pattern throughout your presentation to maintain rapport with these groups. By overlapping representational systems in this way, you help to create a richer experience for all groups.

2. Dovetail participant needs and expectations and work toward achieving your outcome.

   • Use metaphors.
   • Use anchors. Spatial (using particular locations on the stage) and other anchors can be set up to create different states in your audience – curiosity, relaxation, moving toward, moving away from, and so on.

Wrapping up and next steps

1. Wrap up with a strong close:

   • Repeat the presentation's key messages.
   • Integrate your opening points into your closing comments.
   • Obtain commitment or buy-in.
   • Recommend action.

2. Summarize outcome(s) achieved, including time frames and responsibilities.

Appendix A:
Representational Systems Preference Test

THIS PREFERENCE ASSESSMENT may be used for yourself or your friends for your personal enjoyment. It may not be used in articles, presentations, books, manuals, training courses, seminars, workshops or any commercial or business activity without the written permission of Renewal Technologies Inc.

Each of us has a preferred representational system(s), or rep system. The assessment is not fully definitive as there are only twelve questions; as well, your preferred representational system may change over time or in different contexts.

Generally, one representational system is not better than another. If you score low on one or more of the systems, you may wish to become curious and explore how this is affecting your life experiences.

Have fun with this assessment! I hope it provides you with additional insight on how you prefer to communicate with others.

Instructions:
For each of the following statements, please assign a number to every phrase. Use the following system to indicate your preferences:

1 – Least descriptive of you
2 – Next best description
3 – Next best description
4 – Best description of you

If you have trouble deciding between two phrases, go with the first thought that comes to mind.

1. When vacationing at the beach, the first thing that makes me glad to be there is:

a __ The feel of the cool sand, the warm sun or the fresh breeze on my face.

b __ The roar of the waves, the whistling wind or the sound of birds in the distance.

c __ This is the type of vacation that makes sense or the cost is reasonable.

d __ The scenery, the bright sun and the sparkling blue water.

2. When I feel overwhelmed, I find it helps if:

a __ I can see the big picture.

b __ I can talk or listen to another person.

c __ I can get in touch with what is happening.

d __ I make sense of things in my head.

3. When given an assignment at work, it is easier to carry out if:

a __ I can picture what is required.

b __ I have a feeling for what is required.

c __ I have an understanding of what is required.

d __ Someone talks to me about what is required.

4. I find it easier to follow a presentation if:

a __ I feel in touch with the presenter and the material is within my grasp.

b __ There is a visual display so I can visualize the concepts.

c __ The presentation is based on facts and figures and is logically presented.

d __ The presenter speaks clearly with varying tonality or uses sound to emphasize the message.

5. When buying a car, I base my decision on:

a __ The purchase price, gas mileage and safety features.

b __ How comfortable the seats are or the feeling I get when I test drive it.

c __ The color, styling or how I would look in it.

d __ The sound of the engine or stereo system or how quiet it rides.

6. I communicate my thoughts through:

a __ My tone of my voice.

b __ My words.

c __ My appearance.

d __ My feelings.

7. When I am anxious, the first thing that happens is:

a __ Things begin to sound different.
b __ Things begin to feel different.
c __ Things begin to look different.
d __ Things begin to not make sense.

8. During a discussion, I am most influenced by:

a __ The other person's logic and the way the facts are presented.
b __ The other person's tone of voice.
c __ The other person's energy that I feel.
d __ The other person's body language or being able to picture the other person's viewpoint.

9. I assess how well I am doing at work on the basis of:

a __ My understanding of what needs to be done.
b __ How I see myself making progress.
c __ The tone of voice used by my colleagues and superiors.
d __ How satisfied I feel.

10. One of my strengths is my ability to:

a __ See what needs to be done.
b __ Make sense of new facts and data.
c __ Hear what sounds right.
d __ Get in touch with my feelings.

11. It is easiest for me to:

a __ Select the volume, bass and treble for easy listening on a stereo system.
b __ Select an intellectually relevant point in a conversation.
c __ Select comfortable furniture.
d __ Select rich, attractive color combinations.

12. If I agree with someone, I am more likely to say:

a __ That feels right.
b __ That looks right.
c __ That sounds right.
d __ That makes sense.

Determining your preferences:

1. Copy your answers to the lines below:

Question Number	Visual	Auditory	Kinesthetic	Auditory Digital
1	d	b	a	c
2	a	b	c	d
3	a	d	b	c
4	b	d	a	c
5	c	d	b	a
6	c	a	d	b
7	c	a	b	d
8	d	b	c	a
9	b	c	d	a
10	a	c	d	b
11	d	a	c	b
12	b	c	a	d
Total				

2. Add the numbers in each column. A comparison of the totaled scores gives your relative preference for each of the four major representational systems. The higher the score, the higher your preference.

Index

About the Author

ROGER ELLERTON, PhD, CMC is the founder and managing partner of Renewal Technologies Inc. He is an educator, consultant, coach, executive and well-respected speaker, with over thirty years of experience in management, management of change, process renewal, professional and personal development and training.

Roger is a certified trainer in neuro-linguistic programming (NLP), as well as a certified management consultant (CMC) and former executive in the Canadian federal government. He was previously a tenured professor at the University of New Brunswick in Canada, and was listed in the *International Who's Who in Education*.

For over fifteen years, he has been – and continues to be – a student of personal development methodologies. He has written many articles, twelve of which have been published in recognized research journals, and is the co-designer and presenter on the twelve-audiotape series *Change at the Speed of Thought!*

For more information on the seminars, courses, coaching and consulting services that Roger offers, please visit www.renewal.ca.